THIRD EDITION

TOP NOTCH 1

ENGLISH FOR TODAY'S WORLD

JOAN SASLOW
ALLEN ASCHER

With *Top Notch Pop* Songs and Karaoke
by Rob Morsberger

Top Notch: English for Today's World   Level 1, Third Edition

Pearson Education, 10 Bank Street, White Plains, NY 10606 USA

Staff credits: The people who made up the *Top Notch* team are Peter Benson, Kimberly Casey, Jennifer Castro, Tracey Munz Cataldo, Rosa Chapinal, Aerin Csigay, Dave Dickey, Gina DiLillo, Nancy Flaggman, Irene Frankel, Shelley Gazes, Christopher Leonowicz, Julie Molnar, Laurie Neaman, Sherri Pemberton, Pamela Pia, Rebecca Pitke, Jennifer Raspiller, Charlene Straub, and Kenneth Volcjak.

Cover photo: Sprint/Corbis
Text composition: TSI Graphics

Library of Congress Cataloging-in-Publication Data

Saslow, Joan M.
  Top Notch : English for today's world. Fundamentals / Joan Saslow, Allen Ascher ; With Top Notch Pop Songs and Karaoke by Rob Morsberger. — Third Edition.
    pages cm
Includes biographical references.
ISBN 978-0-13-354275-2 — ISBN 978-0-13-339348-4 — ISBN 978-0-13-354277-6 — ISBN 978-0-13-354278-3   1. English language— Textbooks for foreign speakers. 2. English language—Problems, exercises, etc. 3. English language—Sound recordings for foreign speakers.
  I. Ascher, Allen. II. Morsberger, Robert Eustis, 1929- III. Title. IV. Title: English for today's world.
PE1128.S2757 2015
428.2'4--dc23
                          2013044020

Printed in the United States of America
ISBN-10: 0-13-392893-4   ISBN-10: 0-13-339348-8 (with MyEnglishLab)
ISBN-13: 978-0-13-392893-8   ISBN-13: 978-0-13-339348-4 (with MyEnglishLab)
5 17   5 17

pearsonelt.com/topnotch3e

In Memoriam

Rob Morsberger (1959–2013)

The authors wish to acknowledge their memory of and gratitude to **Rob Morsberger**, the gifted composer and songwriter of the *Top Notch Pop* Songs and Karaoke that have provided learners both language practice and pleasure.

ABOUT THE AUTHORS

Joan Saslow

Joan Saslow has taught in a variety of programs in South America and the United States. She is author or coauthor of a number of widely used courses, some of which are *Ready to Go, Workplace Plus, Literacy Plus,* and *Summit.* She is also author of *English in Context,* a series for reading science and technology. Ms. Saslow was the series director of *True Colors* and *True Voices.* She has participated in the English Language Specialist Program in the U.S. Department of State's Bureau of Educational and Cultural Affairs.

Allen Ascher

Allen Ascher has been a teacher and teacher trainer in China and the United States, as well as academic director of the intensive English program at Hunter College. Mr. Ascher has also been an ELT publisher and was responsible for publication and expansion of numerous well-known courses including *True Colors, NorthStar,* the *Longman TOEFL Preparation Series,* and the *Longman Academic Writing Series.* He is coauthor of *Summit,* and he wrote the "Teaching Speaking" module of *Teacher Development Interactive,* an online multimedia teacher-training program.

Ms. Saslow and Mr. Ascher are frequent presenters at professional conferences and have been coauthoring courses for teens, adults, and young adults since 2002.

AUTHORS' ACKNOWLEDGMENTS

The authors are indebted to these reviewers, who provided extensive and detailed feedback and suggestions for *Top Notch,* as well as the hundreds of teachers who completed surveys and participated in focus groups.

Manuel Wilson Alvarado Miles, Quito, Ecuador • **Shirley Ando,** Otemae University, Hyogo, Japan • **Vanessa de Andrade,** CCBEU Inter Americano, Curitiba, Brazil • **Miguel Arrazola,** CBA, Santa Cruz, Bolivia • **Mark Barta,** Proficiency School of English, São Paulo, Brazil • **Edwin Bello,** PROULEX, Guadalajara, Mexico • **Mary Blum,** CBA, Cochabamba, Bolivia • **María Elizabeth Boccia,** Proficiency School of English, São Paulo, Brazil • **Pamela Cristina Borja Baltán,** Quito, Ecuador • **Eliana Anabel L. Buccia,** AMICANA, Mendoza, Argentina • **José Humberto Calderón Díaz,** CALUSAC, Guatemala City, Guatemala • **María Teresa Calienes Csirke,** Idiomas Católica, Lima, Peru • **Esther María Carbo Morales,** Quito, Ecuador • **Jorge Washington Cárdenas Castillo,** Quito, Ecuador • **Eréndira Yadira Carrera García,** UVM Chapultepec, Mexico City, Mexico • **Viviane de Cássia Santos Carlini,** Spectrum Line, Pouso Alegre, Brazil • **Centro Colombo Americano,** Bogota, Colombia • **Guven Ciftci,** Fatih University, Istanbul, Turkey • **Diego Cisneros,** CBA, Tarija, Bolivia • **Paul Crook,** Meisei University, Tokyo, Japan • **Alejandra Díaz Loo,** El Cultural, Arequipa, Peru • **Jesús G. Díaz Osío,** Florida National College, Miami, USA • **María Eid Ceneviva,** CBA, Bolivia • **Amalia Elvira Rodríguez Espinoza De Los Monteros,** Guayaquil, Ecuador • **María Argelia Estrada Vásquez,** CALUSAC, Guatemala City, Guatemala • **John Fieldeldy,** College of Engineering, Nihon University, Aizuwakamatsu-shi, Japan • **Marleni Humbelina Flores Urízar,** CALUSAC, Guatemala City, Guatemala • **Gonzalo Fortune,** CBA, Sucre, Bolivia • **Andrea Fredricks,** Embassy CES, San Francisco, USA • **Irma Gallegos Peláez,** UVM Tlalpan, Mexico City, Mexico • **Alberto Gamarra,** CBA, Santa Cruz, Bolivia • **María Amparo García Peña,** ICPNA Cusco, Peru • **Amanda Gillis-Furutaka,** Kyoto Sangyo University, Kyoto, Japan • **Martha Angelina González**

Párraga, Guayaquil, Ecuador • **Octavio Garduño Ruiz,** Business Training Consultant, Mexico City, Mexico • **Ralph Grayson,** Idiomas Católica, Lima, Peru • **Murat Gultekin,** Fatih University, Istanbul, Turkey • **Oswaldo Gutiérrez,** PROULEX, Guadalajara, Mexico • **Ayaka Hashinishi,** Otemae University, Hyogo, Japan • **Alma Lorena Hernández de Armas,** CALUSAC, Guatemala City, Guatemala • **Kent Hill,** Seigakuin University, Saitama-ken, Japan • **Kayoko Hirao,** Nichii Gakkan Company, COCO Juku, Japan • **Jesse Huang,** National Central University, Taoyuan, Taiwan • **Eric Charles Jones,** Seoul University of Technology, Seoul, South Korea • **Jun-Chen Kuo,** Tajen University, Pingtung , Taiwan • **Susan Krieger,** Embassy CES, San Francisco, USA • **Ana María de la Torre Ugarte,** ICPNA Chiclayo, Peru • **Erin Lemaistre,** Chung-Ang University, Seoul, South Korea • **Eleanor S. Leu,** Soochow University, Taipei, Taiwan • **Yihui Li (Stella Li),** Fooyin University, Kaohsiung, Taiwan • **Chin-Fan Lin,** Shih Hsin University, Taipei, Taiwan • **Linda Lin,** Tatung Institute of Technology, Taiwan • **Kristen Lindblom,** Embassy CES, San Francisco, USA • **Patricio David López Logacho,** Quito, Ecuador • **Diego López Tasara,** Idiomas Católica, Lima, Peru • **Neil Macleod,** Kansai Gaidai University, Osaka, Japan • **Adriana Marcés,** Idiomas Católica, Lima, Peru • **Robyn McMurray,** Pusan National University, Busan, South Korea • **Paula Medina,** London Language Institute, London, Canada • **Juan Carlos Muñoz,** American School Way, Bogota, Colombia • **Noriko Mori,** Otemae University, Hyogo, Japan • **Adrián Esteban Narváez Pacheco,** Cuenca, Ecuador • **Tim Newfields,** Tokyo University Faculty of Economics, Tokyo, Japan • **Ana Cristina Ochoa,** CCBEU Inter Americano, Curitiba, Brazil • **Tania Elizabeth Ortega Santacruz,** Cuenca, Ecuador • **Martha Patricia Páez,** Quito, Ecuador • **María de Lourdes Pérez Valdespino,** Universidad del Valle

de México, Mexico • **Wahrena Elizabeth Pfeister,** University of Suwon, Gyeonggi-Do, South Korea • **Wayne Allen Pfeister,** University of Suwon, Gyeonggi-Do, South Korea • **Andrea Rebonato,** CCBEU Inter Americano, Curitiba, Brazil • **Thomas Robb,** Kyoto Sangyo University, Kyoto, Japan • **Mehran Sabet,** Seigakuin University, Saitama-ken, Japan • **Majid Safadaran Mosazadeh,** ICPNA Chiclayo, Peru • **Timothy Samuelson,** BridgeEnglish, Denver, USA • **Héctor Sánchez,** PROULEX, Guadalajara, Mexico • **Mónica Alexandra Sánchez Escalante,** Quito, Ecuador • **Jorge Mauricio Sánchez Montalván,** Quito, Universidad Politécnica Salesiana (UPS), Ecuador • **Letícia Santos,** ICBEU Ibiá, Brazil • **Elena Sapp,** INTO Oregon State University, Corvallis, USA • **Robert Sheridan,** Otemae University, Hyogo, Japan • **John Eric Sherman,** Hong Ik University, Seoul, South Korea • **Brooks Slaybaugh,** Asia University, Tokyo, Japan • **João Vitor Soares,** NACC, São Paulo, Brazil • **Silvia Solares,** CBA, Sucre, Bolivia • **Chayawan Sonchaeng,** Delaware County Community College, Media, PA • **María Julia Suárez,** CBA, Cochabamba, Bolivia • **Elena Sudakova,** English Language Center, Kiev, Ukraine • **Richard Swingle,** Kansai Gaidai College, Osaka, Japan • **Blanca Luz Terrazas Zamora,** ICPNA Cusco, Peru • **Sandrine Ting,** St. John's University, New Taipei City, Taiwan • **Christian Juan Torres Medina,** Guayaquil, Ecuador • **Raquel Torrico,** CBA, Sucre, Bolivia • **Jessica Ueno,** Otemae University, Hyogo, Japan • **Ximena Vacaflor C.,** CBA, Tarija, Bolivia • **René Valdivia Pereira,** CBA, Santa Cruz, Bolivia • **Solange Lopes Vinagre Costa,** SENAC, São Paulo, Brazil • **Magno Alejandro Vivar Hurtado,** Cuenca, Ecuador • **Dr. Wen-hsien Yang,** National Kaohsiung Hospitality College, Kaohsiung, Taiwan • **Juan Zárate,** El Cultural, Arequipa, Peru

LEARNING OBJECTIVES

Top Notch 1 learning objectives are designed for false beginners. They offer a rigorous review and an expansion of key beginning concepts as well as a wealth of new and challenging material.

	COMMUNICATION GOALS	VOCABULARY	GRAMMAR

UNIT 1
Getting Acquainted
PAGE 2
	• Meet someone new
	• Identify and describe people
	• Provide personal information
	• Introduce someone to a group
		• Formal titles
		• Positive adjectives to describe people
		• Personal information
		• Countries and nationalities
			• Information questions with <u>be</u>: Review
			• Contractions
			• Modification with adjectives: Review
			• Positive adjectives
			• Yes / <u>no</u> questions and short answers with <u>be</u>: Review
			
			GRAMMAR BOOSTER
			  • Information questions with <u>be</u>: usage and form
			  • Possessive nouns and adjectives
			  • Verb <u>be</u>: usage and form
			  • Short answers with <u>be</u>: common errors

UNIT 2
Going Out
PAGE 14
	• Accept or decline an invitation
	• Express locations and give directions
	• Make plans to see an event
	• Talk about musical tastes
		• Music genres
		• Entertainment and cultural events
		• Locations and directions
			• Prepositions of time and place; Questions with <u>When</u>, <u>What time</u>, and <u>Where</u>: Review
			• Contractions
			
			GRAMMAR BOOSTER
			  • Prepositions of time and place: usage rules
			  • <u>Would like</u> for preference: review and expansion

UNIT 3
The Extended Family
PAGE 26
	• Report news about relationships
	• Describe extended families
	• Compare people
	• Discuss family cultural traditions
		• The extended family
		• Relationships and marital status
		• Other family relationships
		• Similarities and differences
			• The simple present tense: Review
			• Spelling exceptions
			• Contractions
			• The simple present tense—information questions: Review
			
			GRAMMAR BOOSTER
			  • The simple present tense: usage and form
			  • Information questions in the simple present tense: form questions with <u>who</u>, common errors

UNIT 4
Food and Restaurants
PAGE 38
	• Ask for a restaurant recommendation
	• Order from a menu
	• Speak to a server and pay for a meal
	• Discuss food and health
		• Parts of a meal
		• Categories of food
		• Degrees of hunger
		• Communicating with a waiter or waitress
		• Adjectives to describe the healthfulness of food
			• <u>There is</u> and <u>there are</u> with count and non-count nouns; <u>Anything</u> and <u>nothing</u>
			• Definite article <u>the</u>
			
			GRAMMAR BOOSTER
			  • Non-count nouns: expressing quantities
			  • <u>Some</u> and <u>any</u>
			  • Questions with <u>How much</u> and <u>How many</u>
			  • Words that can be count nouns or non-count nouns
			  • Plural count nouns: spelling rules
			  • Non-count nouns: categories and verb agreement

UNIT 5
Technology and You
PAGE 50
	• Recommend a brand or model
	• Express sympathy for a problem
	• Complain when things don't work
	• Describe features of products
		• Electronic devices
		• Replacing products
		• Positive descriptions
		• Collocations for using electronic devices
		• Activities
		• Ways to sympathize
		• Negative descriptions
		• Household appliances and machines
		• Ways to state a problem
		• Features of manufactured products
			• The present continuous: Review
			
			GRAMMAR BOOSTER
			  • The present continuous: spelling rules for the present participle
			  • The present continuous: rules for forming statements
			  • The present continuous: rules for forming questions

CONVERSATION STRATEGIES	LISTENING / PRONUNCIATION	READING	WRITING
• Begin responses with a question to confirm • Use <u>Let's</u> to suggest a course of action • Ask personal questions to indicate friendliness • Intensify an informal answer with <u>sure</u>	**Listening Skills** • Listen for details • Infer information **Pronunciation** • Intonation of questions	**Texts** • An enrollment form • Personal profiles • A photo story **Skills/strategies** • Infer information • Scan for facts	**Task** • Write a description of a classmate **WRITING BOOSTER** • Capitalization
• "Use <u>Would you like to go?</u>" to make an invitation • Repeat with rising intonation to confirm information • Provide reasons to decline an invitation • Use <u>Too bad</u> to express disappointment • Use <u>Thanks, anyway</u> to acknowledge an unsuccessful attempt to help	**Listening Skills** • Listen for key details • Draw conclusions • Listen for details • Listen for locations **Pronunciation** • Rising intonation to confirm information	**Texts** • A music website • An entertainment events page • Authentic interviews • A survey of musical tastes • A photo story **Skills/strategies** • Interpret maps and diagrams • Confirm content • Make personal comparisons	**Task** • Write about oneself and one's musical tastes **WRITING BOOSTER** • The sentence
• Use <u>Actually</u> to introduce a topic • Respond to good news with <u>Congratulations!</u> • Respond to bad news with <u>I'm sorry to hear that</u> • Use <u>Thanks for asking</u> to acknowledge an inquiry of concern • Use <u>Well</u> to introduce a lengthy reply • Ask follow-up questions to keep a conversation going	**Listening Skills** • Listen to classify • Listen to infer • Listen to identify similarities and differences • Listen to take notes • Listen for details **Pronunciation** • Linking sounds	**Texts** • Family tree diagrams • A self-help website • A survey about adult children • A photo story **Skills/strategies** • Interpret a diagram • Confirm facts • Infer information	**Task** • Make a Venn diagram • Compare two people in a family **WRITING BOOSTER** • Combining sentences with <u>and</u> or <u>but</u>
• Use <u>Could you . . . ?</u> to make a polite request • Use <u>Sure</u> to agree to a request • Clarify a request by asking for more specific information • Indicate a sudden thought with <u>Actually</u> • Use <u>I'll have</u> to order from a server • Increase politeness with <u>please</u>	**Listening Skills** • Listen to take notes • Listen to predict • Infer the location of a conversation **Pronunciation** • <u>The</u> before consonant and vowel sounds	**Texts** • Menus • A nutrition website • A photo story **Skills/strategies** • Interpret a map • Understand from context • Infer information	**Task** • Write a short article about food for a travel blog **WRITING BOOSTER** • Connecting words and ideas: <u>and</u> or <u>in addition</u>
• Use <u>Hey</u> or <u>How's it going</u> for an informal greeting • Use <u>What about . . . ?</u> to offer a suggestion • Use <u>Really?</u> to indicate surprise • Use <u>You know</u> to introduce a topic • Express sympathy when someone is frustrated	**Listening Skills** • Infer meaning • Listen to predict • Listen for details • Listen to classify **Pronunciation** • Intonation of questions	**Texts** • Newspaper advertisements • An online review for a product • A photo story **Skills/strategies** • Understand from context • Activate language from a text	**Task** • Write a review of a product **WRITING BOOSTER** • Placement of adjectives: before nouns and after the verb <u>be</u>

	COMMUNICATION GOALS	VOCABULARY	GRAMMAR
UNIT 6 **Staying in Shape** PAGE 62	• Plan an activity with someone • Talk about habitual activities and future plans • Discuss fitness and eating habits • Describe your routines	• Physical activities • Places for sports and exercise • Frequency adverbs	• Can and have to • The present continuous and the simple present tense: Review GRAMMAR BOOSTER • Can and have to: form and common errors • Can and have to: information questions • Can and be able to: present and past forms • The simple present tense: non-action verbs • The simple present tense: placement of frequency adverbs • Time expressions
UNIT 7 **On Vacation** PAGE 74	• Greet someone arriving from a trip • Ask about someone's vacation • Discuss vacation preferences • Describe good and bad vacation experiences	• Adjectives to describe trips • Intensifiers • Decline and accept help • Adjectives for vacations • Bad and good travel experiences	• The past tense of be: Review • Contractions • The simple past tense: Review • Regular and irregular verb forms GRAMMAR BOOSTER • The past tense of be: form • The simple past tense: spelling rules for regular verbs • The simple past tense: usage and form
UNIT 8 **Shopping for Clothes** PAGE 86	• Shop and pay for clothes • Ask for a different size or color • Navigate a mall or department store • Discuss clothing do's and don'ts	• Clothes and clothing departments • Types of clothing and shoes • Formal clothes • Clothing that comes in "pairs" • Store departments • Clothing sizes • Interior store locations and directions • Prepositions of interior location • Formality and appropriateness in clothing	• Uses of object pronouns • Subject and object pronouns • Comparative adjectives GRAMMAR BOOSTER • Direct objects: usage • Indirect objects: usage rules and common errors • Comparative adjectives: spelling rules
UNIT 9 **Taking Transportation** PAGE 98	• Discuss schedules and buy tickets • Book travel services • Understand airport announcements • Describe transportation problems	• Kinds of tickets and trips • Ways to express disappointment • Travel services • Airline passenger information • Some flight problems • Transportation problems • Means of transportation	• Modals should and could • Be going to + base form to express the future: Review GRAMMAR BOOSTER • Modals can, could, and should: meaning, form, and common errors • Expansion: future actions
UNIT 10 **Spending Money** PAGE 110	• Ask for a recommendation • Bargain for a lower price • Discuss showing appreciation for service • Describe where to get the best deals	• Financial terms • How to bargain • How to describe good and bad deals	• Superlative adjectives • Irregular forms • Too and enough GRAMMAR BOOSTER • Comparative and superlative adjectives: usage and form • Intensifiers very, really, and too

CONVERSATION STRATEGIES	LISTENING / PRONUNCIATION	READING	WRITING
• Use <u>Why don't we . . . ?</u> to suggest an activity • Say <u>Sorry, I can't</u> to apologize for turning down an invitation • Provide a reason with <u>have to</u> to decline an invitation • Use <u>Well, how about . . . ?</u> to suggest an alternative • Use <u>How come?</u> to ask for a reason • Use a negative question to confirm information	**Listening Skills** • Listen to activate grammar • Listen for main ideas • Listen for details • Apply and personalize information **Pronunciation** • <u>Can</u> / <u>can't</u> • Third-person singular –s: Review	**Texts** • A bar graph • A fitness survey • A magazine article • A photo story **Skills/strategies** • Interpret a bar graph • Infer information • Summarize	**Task** • Write about one's exercise and health habits **WRITING BOOSTER** • Punctuation of statements and questions
• Say <u>Welcome back!</u> to indicate enthusiasm about someone's return from a trip • Acknowledge someone's interest with <u>Actually</u> • Decline an offer of assistance with <u>It's OK. I'm fine.</u> • Confirm that an offer is declined with <u>Are you sure?</u> • Use <u>Absolutely</u> to confirm a response • Show enthusiasm with <u>No kidding!</u> and <u>Tell me more.</u>	**Listening Skills** • Listen for main ideas • Listen for details • Infer meaning **Pronunciation** • The simple past tense ending: Regular verbs	**Texts** • Travel brochures • Personal travel stories • A vacation survey • A photo story **Skills/strategies** • Activate language from a text • Identify supporting details • Support an opinion • Draw conclusions	**Task** Write a guided essay about a vacation **WRITING BOOSTER** • Time order
• Use <u>Excuse me</u> to indicate you didn't understand or couldn't hear • Use <u>Excuse me</u> to begin a conversation with a clerk • Follow a question with more information for clarification • Acknowledge someone's assistance with <u>Thanks for your help</u> • Respond to gratitude with <u>My pleasure</u>	**Listening Skills** • Infer the appropriate location • Understand locations and directions **Pronunciation** • Contrastive stress for clarification	**Texts** • An online clothing catalogue • Simple and complex diagrams and plans • A travel article • A personal opinion survey • A photo story **Skills/strategies** • Identify supporting details • Paraphrase • Apply information	**Task** • Write a letter or e-mail explaining what clothes to pack **WRITING BOOSTER** • Connecting ideas with <u>because</u> and <u>since</u>
• Use <u>I'm sorry</u> to respond with disappointing information • Use <u>Well</u> to introduce an alternative • Use <u>I hope so</u> to politely respond to an offer of help • Use <u>Let me check</u> to buy time to get information	**Listening Skills** • Infer the type of travel service • Understand public announcements • Listen for details • Use reasoning to evaluate statements of fact **Pronunciation** • Intonation for offering alternatives	**Texts** • Transportation schedules • Public transportation tickets • Arrival and departure boards • Magazine and newspaper articles • A photo story **Skills/strategies** • Make decisions based on schedules and needs • Critical thinking	**Task** • Write about two different trips, one past trip and one future trip **WRITING BOOSTER** • The paragraph
• Use <u>Well</u> to connect an answer to an earlier question • Use <u>How about . . . ?</u> to make a financial offer • Use <u>OK</u> to indicate that an agreement has been reached	**Listening Skills** • Listen for key details • Listen for main ideas • Listen for details **Pronunciation** • Rising intonation for clarification	**Texts** • A travel guide • Product ads • A magazine article • Personal travel stories • A photo story **Skills/strategies** • Classify information • Draw conclusions • Apply information	**Task** • Write a guide to your city, including information on where to stay, visit, and shop **WRITING BOOSTER** • Connecting contradictory ideas: <u>even though</u>, <u>however</u>, <u>on the other hand</u>

TO THE TEACHER

What is *Top Notch?* *Top Notch* is a six-level* communicative course that prepares adults and young adults to interact successfully and confidently with both native and non-native speakers of English.

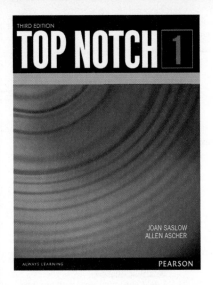

The goal of *Top Notch* is to make English unforgettable through:
- Multiple exposures to new language
- Numerous opportunities to practice it
- Deliberate and intensive recycling

The *Top Notch* course has two beginning levels—*Top Notch Fundamentals* for true beginners and *Top Notch 1* for false beginners. *Top Notch* is benchmarked to the Global Scale of English and is tightly correlated to the Can-do Statements of the Common European Framework of Reference.

Each full level of *Top Notch* contains material for 60–90 hours of classroom instruction. In addition, the entire course can be tailored to blended learning with an integrated online component, *MyEnglishLab*.

NEW This third edition of *Top Notch* includes these new features: Extra Grammar Exercises, digital full-color Vocabulary Flash Cards, Conversation Activator videos, and Pronunciation Coach videos.

* *Summit 1* and *Summit 2* are the titles of the 5th and 6th levels of the *Top Notch* course.

Award-Winning Instructional Design*

Daily confirmation of progress

Each easy-to-follow two-page lesson begins with a clearly stated practical communication goal closely aligned to the Common European Framework's Can-do Statements. All activities are integrated with the goal, giving vocabulary and grammar meaning and purpose. *Now You Can* activities ensure that students achieve each goal and confirm their progress in every class session.

Explicit vocabulary and grammar

Clear captioned picture-dictionary illustrations with accompanying audio take the guesswork out of meaning and pronunciation. Grammar presentations containing both rules and examples clarify form, meaning, and use. The unique *Recycle this Language* feature continually puts known words and grammar in front of students' eyes as they communicate, to make sure language remains active.

High-frequency social language

Twenty memorable conversation models provide appealing natural social language that students can carry "in their pockets" for use in real life. Rigorous controlled and free discussion activities systematically stimulate recycling of social language, ensuring that it's not forgotten.

Linguistic and cultural fluency

Top Notch equips students to interact with people from different language backgrounds by including authentic accents on the audio. Conversation Models, Photo Stories, and cultural fluency activities prepare students for social interactions in English with people from unfamiliar cultures.

Active listening syllabus

All Vocabulary presentations, Pronunciation presentations, Conversation Models, Photo Stories, Listening Comprehension exercises, and Readings are recorded on the audio to help students develop good pronunciation, intonation, and auditory memory. In addition, approximately fifty carefully developed listening tasks at each level of *Top Notch* develop crucial listening comprehension skills such as listen for details, listen for main ideas, listen to activate vocabulary, listen to activate grammar, and listen to confirm information.

We wish you and your students enjoyment and success with **Top Notch 1.** *We wrote it for you.*

Joan Saslow and Allen Ascher

* *Top Notch* is the recipient of the Association of Educational Publishers' *Distinguished Achievement Award.*

ActiveTeach

Maximize the impact of your *Top Notch* lessons. This digital tool provides an interactive classroom experience that can be used with or without an interactive whiteboard (IWB). It includes a full array of digital and printable features.

For class presentation . . .

- **NEW** Conversation Activator videos: increase students' confidence in oral communication
- **NEW** Pronunciation Coach videos: facilitate clear and fluent oral expression
- **NEW** Extra Grammar Exercises: ensure mastery of grammar
- **V** **NEW** Digital Full-Color Vocabulary Flash Cards: accelerate retention of new vocabulary

PLUS

- ▶ Clickable Audio: instant access to the complete classroom audio program
- *Top Notch TV* Video Program: a hilarious sitcom and authentic on-the-street interviews
- *Top Notch Pop* Songs and Karaoke: original songs for additional language practice

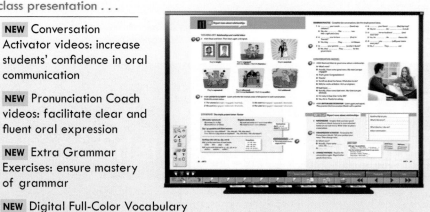

For planning . . .

- A *Methods Handbook* for a communicative classroom
- Detailed timed lesson plans for each two-page lesson
- *Top Notch TV* teaching notes
- Complete answer keys, audio scripts, and video scripts

For extra support . . .

- Hundreds of extra printable activities, with teaching notes
- *Top Notch Pop* language exercises
- *Top Notch TV* activity worksheets

For assessment . . .

- Ready-made unit and review achievement tests with options to edit, add, or delete items.

MyEnglishLab

An optional online learning tool

- **NEW** Grammar Coach videos, plus the Pronunciation Coach videos, and Digital Vocabulary Flash Cards
- **NEW** Immediate and meaningful feedback on wrong answers
- **NEW** Remedial grammar exercises
- Interactive practice of all material presented in the course
- Grade reports that display performance and time on task
- Auto-graded achievement tests

Workbook

Lesson-by-lesson written exercises to accompany the Student's Book

Full-Course Placement Tests

Choose printable or online version

Classroom Audio Program

- A set of Audio CDs, as an alternative to the clickable audio in the ActiveTeach
- Contains a variety of authentic regional and non-native accents to build comprehension of diverse English speakers
- **NEW** The entire audio program is available for students at www.english.com/topnotch3e. The mobile app *Top Notch Go* allows access anytime, anywhere and lets students practice at their own pace.

Teacher's Edition and Lesson Planner

- Detailed interleaved lesson plans, language and culture notes, answer keys, and more
- Also accessible in digital form in the ActiveTeach

For more information: www.pearsonelt.com/topnotch3e

COMMUNICATION GOALS

1 Meet someone new.
2 Identify and describe people.
3 Provide personal information.
4 Introduce someone to a group.

PREVIEW

English and You!
Why are you learning English?

☐ for business

☐ for travel

☐ for my studies

☐ to get to know people who don't speak my language

☐ other:.....................................

Did You Know?

There are 2 billion (2,000,000,000) English speakers around the world. Fewer than twenty percent (20%) are native speakers of English.

Please complete the form.

Title: ☐ Mr. ☐ Mrs. ☐ Ms. ☐ Miss

Last/Family Name   First/Given Name

Nationality

Occupation

A **PAIR WORK** Why are you learning English? Compare reasons with a partner.

B **CLASS SURVEY** How many students in your class are studying English . . .

.... for business?   .... for their studies?   .... (other reasons)

.... for travel?   .... to get to know people?

C ▶1:02 **PHOTO STORY** Read and listen to people getting acquainted.

Susan: I'll bet this is your dad.
Cara: Yes, it is. Dad, I'd like you to meet my friend, Susan Grant.
Sam: It's a pleasure to meet you, Susan. Samuel Pike.
Susan: Great to meet you, too. But please, everyone calls me by my nickname, Suzy.

Sam: And just call me Sam. So, what do you do, Suzy?
Susan: I'm a photographer . . . Oh, I'm sorry. There's my husband . . . Ted, over here!

Ted: Sorry I'm late.
Susan: Ted, this is Cara's dad.
Ted: Oh, how nice to meet you, Mr. Pike!
Sam: Likewise. But please call me Sam.

D **FOCUS ON LANGUAGE** Look at the underlined expressions in the Photo Story. With a partner, find:

1 two ways to introduce people.

2 three ways to greet new people.

3 three ways to tell others they can be informal.

> ▶1:03 **Formal titles**
> | Men | Women |
> |---|---|
> | Mr. | **Ms.** (married or single) |
> | | **Mrs.** (married) |
> | | **Miss** (single) |
>
> Use titles with family names, not given names.
> Ms. Grant NOT ~~Ms. Suzy~~
>
> **Marital status**
>
> married = 🧑‍🤝‍🧑   single = 🚫

SPEAKING

A Complete your response to each person. Write the correct formal titles.

Nice to meet you.

GIVEN NAME *Marc*
FAMILY NAME *Anthony*
OCCUPATION *singer*

Good to meet you.

GIVEN NAME *Jennifer*
FAMILY NAME *Lawrence*
OCCUPATION *actor*

1 Good to meet you, too, ... !
   (Mr. Marc / Mr. Anthony / Ms. Anthony)

2 Nice to meet you, too, ... !
   (Ms. Lawrence / Ms. Jennifer / Mr. Lawrence)

B **ROLE PLAY** Imagine your partner is a famous person. Introduce your partner to the class. Use formal titles.

❝ I'd like you to meet Bradley Cooper. Mr. Cooper is an actor. ❞

GOAL Meet someone new

CONVERSATION MODEL

A ▶1:04 Read and listen to people meeting someone new.

A: Who's that?

B: Over there? I think she's new.

A: Well, let's say hello.

• • •

B: Good morning. I'm Alex, and this is Lauren.

C: Hi. My name's Kathryn Gao. But everyone calls me Kate.

A: Great to meet you, Kate. Where are you from?

C: New York.

B ▶1:05 **RHYTHM AND INTONATION** Listen again and repeat. Then practice the Conversation Model with a partner.

GRAMMAR *Information questions with be: Review*

Who's Ms. Nieto?	She's my teacher.
Who are they?	They're my classmates.
Where's she from?	She's from Seoul, Korea.
What city are you from?	We're from Los Angeles.
What's your occupation?	I'm an engineer.
What's his e-mail address?	It's ted@kr.com [say "ted at k-r-dot-com"].
What are their names?	Andrea and Steven.
How old is your brother?	He's twenty-six.
How old are they?	She's twelve, and her little sister is eight.

Contractions

Who's = Who is	**I'm** = I am	**you're** = you are
Where's = Where is	**he's** = he is	**we're** = we are
What's = What is	**she's** = she is	**they're** = they are
	it's = it is	

GRAMMAR BOOSTER p. 123
- Information questions with be: usage and form
- Possessive nouns and adjectives

A **GRAMMAR PRACTICE** Complete the conversations. Use contractions of the verb be when possible.

1 A: .... that over there?

B: Oh, that's Hasna. .... from Lebanon.

A: .... she? She looks very young.

B: I think .... twenty-five.

2 A: Your new neighbor's good-looking! .... his name?

B: His name's Francisco.

A: .... he from?

B: El Salvador.

3 A: .... they?

   B: I think .... new students.

   A: .... their names?

   B: Evan and Kim.

4 A: It was nice to meet your brothers. .... they?

   B: Greg's only fourteen. But my older brother, David, is twenty-eight.

   A: .... David's occupation?

   B: .... a lawyer.

5 A: I'll call you sometime. .... your phone number?

   B: .... 555-0296. .... yours?

   A: 555-8747.

6 A: .... your e-mail address? I'll send you a note.

   B: .... choi23@kr.com.

   A: K - r - dot - com? That's interesting. .... you from?

   B: Busan, Korea. I'm here on business.

DIGITAL MORE EXERCISES

B **GRAMMAR PRACTICE** Write at least four information questions for your partner. Begin each question with a capital letter and end with a question mark.

What's your phone number?

Ideas
Who . . . ?
What . . . ?
Where . . . ?
How old . . . ?

Audrey Miller
cell: (415) 555-8393
e-mail:
audreym@pnet.com

C **PAIR WORK** Now ask your questions, and answer your partner's questions.

NOW YOU CAN   Meet someone new

DIGITAL VIDEO

A **CONVERSATION ACTIVATOR** With two partners, personalize the Conversation Model. Imagine one of you is new to your school, office, or neighborhood. Meet that person. Then change roles.

A: Who .... ?

B: Over there? I think .... new.

A: Well, let's say hello.

   . . .

B: .... I'm .... , and this is ....

C: .... My name's ....

A: .... Where are you from?

C: ....

DON'T STOP!
Ask more questions.
What city are you from?
What's your occupation?
Who's your teacher?

RECYCLE THIS LANGUAGE.

Introduce people	Greet new people	Shift to informality
This is __.	Great to meet you.	Everyone calls me __.
I'd like you to meet __.	How nice to meet you!	Please call me __.
	It's a pleasure to meet you.	Just call me __.

B **CHANGE PARTNERS** Practice the conversation again. Meet other people.

GOAL Identify and describe people

GRAMMAR *Modification with adjectives: Review*

Adjectives describe nouns and pronouns. They can go after the verb <u>be</u> or before a noun.

Usain Bolt is terrific. He's a terrific athlete from Jamaica.
Tony Leung and Gong Li are famous. They're famous actors from China. They're wonderful.

Use an article before an adjective that modifies a singular noun.

He's a great musician. NOT ~~He's great musician.~~

▶1:06 **Positive adjectives**

beautiful	handsome
famous	terrific
fantastic	wonderful
great	

A **GRAMMAR PRACTICE** Combine each pair of sentences.

1 Chris Pine is an actor from the U.S. He's handsome.

2 Emeli Sandé is a singer from the U.K. She's fantastic.

3 Cheng Fei and Yao Jinnan are athletes from China. They're terrific.

4 Sebastião Salgado is a photographer from Brazil. He's great.

5 Alice Munro is a writer from Canada. She's famous.

Chris Pine is a handsome actor from the U.S.

B Now write three sentences about other famous people. Use an adjective before a noun.

DIGITAL
MORE
EXERCISES

CONVERSATION MODEL

A ▶1:07 Read and listen to someone identify and describe a person.

A: Hey. Who's Lucia Micarelli?

B: You don't know? For real?

A: No. Is she famous?

B: She sure is. She's a great musician.

A: Where's she from?

B: The United States.

B ▶1:08 **RHYTHM AND INTONATION** Listen again and repeat. Then practice the Conversation Model with a partner.

GRAMMAR *Yes / <u>no</u> questions and short answers with <u>be</u>: Review*

Are you our teacher?	Yes, I am.	No, I'm not.
Is she Chinese?	Yes, she is.	No, she isn't. [No, she's not.]
Is your nickname Josh?	Yes, it is.	No, it isn't. [No, it's not.]
Are you and Tom students?	Yes, we are.	No, we aren't. [No, we're not.]
Are they famous?	Yes, they are.	No, they aren't. [No, they're not.]

Be careful!
Yes, I am. NOT ~~Yes, I'm.~~
Yes, she is. NOT ~~Yes, she's.~~

GRAMMAR BOOSTER p. 124
• Verb <u>be</u>: usage and form
• Short answers with <u>be</u>: common errors

A **FIND THE GRAMMAR** Find and underline two information questions and one yes / no question with <u>be</u> in the Conversation Model on page 6.

B **GRAMMAR PRACTICE** Complete the questions and answers. Use contractions when possible.

1 A: .... your father a teacher?
B: Yes, ...

2 A: .... your son an athlete?
B: No, ... an artist.

3 A: .... this your new address?
B: Yes, ...

4 A: Who .... those new students?
.... from Canada?
B: No, ... I think ....
from the U.K.

5 A: That's a nice hat! .... new?
B: No, ...

6 A: .... you a musician?
B: Yes, ... a violinist.

PRONUNCIATION *Intonation of questions*

A ▶1:09 Use rising intonation in yes / no questions. Use falling intonation in information questions. Read and listen. Then listen again and repeat.

Yes / no questions	**Information questions**
Is she an architect?	What's her occupation?
Are they from Canada?	Where are they from?

B **PAIR WORK** Write three yes / no questions and three information questions with <u>be</u>. Begin each question with a capital letter and end with a question mark. Then take turns practicing question intonation.

NOW YOU CAN Identify and describe people

A Look at the famous people. Add information about a famous person you know.

B **CONVERSATION ACTIVATOR** With a partner, change the Conversation Model. Practice identifying and describing famous people. Use an adjective from the Grammar on page 6. Then change roles.

A: Hey. Who's .... ?
B: You don't know? For real?
A: No. Is .... famous?
B: .... sure is. .... 's a ....
A: Where .... from?
B: ....

C **CHANGE PARTNERS** Practice the conversation again. Talk about other famous people. Use other adjectives.

Javier Bardem
actor (Spain)

Jeanne Gang
architect (U.S.)

Angélique Kidjo
singer (Benin)

Your own famous person
first name ....
last name ....
occupation ....
country ....
adjective to describe the person
....

BEFORE YOU LISTEN

A ▶1:10 **VOCABULARY** • *Personal information*
Read and listen. Then listen again and repeat.

nationality   He's originally from India, but his **nationality** is Canadian. He has a Canadian passport.

birthplace   I'm from Mexico City, but it isn't my **birthplace**. I was born in a beautiful small town called Patzcuaro.

hometown   She was born in Seoul, but her **hometown** is Busan. She grew up there.

▶1:11 **Countries and nationalities**

Country	Nationality
I'm from **Japan**.	I'm **Japanese**.
She's from **China**.	She's **Chinese**.
She's from **Canada**.	She's **Canadian**.
They're from **Argentina**.	They're **Argentinean**.
He's from the **U.K.**	He's **British**.
We're from **Turkey**.	We're **Turkish**.

See page 122 for a more complete list.

B   **PAIR WORK**   Ask your partner questions, using the Vocabulary.

❝ What's your birthplace? ❞

LISTENING COMPREHENSION

A ▶1:12 **LISTEN FOR DETAILS**   Listen to each conversation and write each person's nationality and occupation. Then check <u>yes</u> or <u>no</u> to indicate whether the person has a nickname.

	Nationality	Occupation	Nickname?	
1			☐ yes	☐ no
2			☐ yes	☐ no
3			☐ yes	☐ no
4			☐ yes	☐ no

a computer programmer

an interpreter

a graphic designer

a salesperson

B ▶1:13 **LISTEN TO INFER**   Now listen to each conversation again and complete each statement.

1 He grew up in ....
  a Ankara **b** London **c** Izmir

2 Her birthplace is ....
  a Osaka **b** Tokyo **c** Seoul

3 She's originally from ....
  a Buenos Aires **b** Montevideo **c** Santiago

4 His hometown is ....
  a Chicago **b** Toronto **c** New York

Provide personal information

INFORMATION GAP

Partner A: Look at the top of the page.
Partner B: Turn your book and look at the bottom of the page.
Ask information questions with <u>be</u> and write the missing
personal information.

PARTNER A

Name: Gordon Graham
Nickname: Gordy
Occupation: ....
Nationality: Australian
Hometown: Canberra
Birthplace: ....
Age: ....
E-mail: gordyg@umail.com.au

Name: ....
Nickname: ....
Occupation: salesperson
Nationality: ....
Age: 36
Hometown: ....
E-mail: beto.wilson@vmail.com.cl

Name: ....
Occupation: scientist
Age: ....
Nationality: Japanese
Hometown: Osaka
E-mail: ....

Name: Claire Beti
Occupation: ....
Age: 24
Nationality: ....
Hometown: ....
Birthplace: Cameroon
E-mail: claire.pokou@inet.com.fr

Name: ....
Occupation: writer
Age: ....
Nationality: French
Hometown: Paris
Birthplace: ....
E-mail: ....

Name: Miya Kato
Occupation: ....
Age: 30
Nationality: ....
Hometown: ....
E-mail: mkato@unet.com.jp

Name: Alberto Wilson
Nickname: Beto
Occupation: ....
Nationality: Chilean
Age: ....
Hometown: Santiago
E-mail: ....

Name: ....
Nickname: ....
Occupation: architect
Nationality: ....
Hometown: ....
Birthplace: Sydney
Age: 24
E-mail: ....

PARTNER B

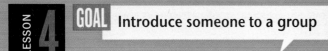

BEFORE YOU READ

A **WARM-UP** In your life, where do you see or hear English?

B **PREVIEW** Before you read, search for the word <u>English</u> in the article. Then answer this question: How does each person use English?

READING ▶ 1:14

Who Uses English?

THIS IS MITSUHIKO TANAKA, a computer programmer at an international publishing company in Japan. He is originally from Sendai, but he works at his company's offices in Tokyo now, where he lives with his wife, Tomiko, and their young son, Hiro. "English is very important in our work. We use it to communicate with colleagues who speak many different languages at our offices all over the world," says Mr. Tanaka. "We also get visitors several times each year, so we use English for our meetings." At home, Mr. Tanaka gets new ideas about computing from websites in English on the Internet. He also uses his English in social media to keep in touch with friends all over the world.

MEET LETICIA MARQUES. She works as a financial manager for a Swedish automotive company in Curitiba, Brazil, where she was born and raised. She is single and lives with her parents. "I use English every day," Ms. Marques says. "We use it in most of our e-mails and meetings and for calls to Sweden, the U.S., and France." In her free time, she likes to watch movies in English. "It's good for my pronunciation," she says.

THIS IS HAMZA ITANI, an executive assistant at a four-star hotel in Dubai, in the United Arab Emirates. Mr. Itani lives in Dubai now, but his hometown is the city of Beirut, in Lebanon. At his job in Dubai, he uses English every day. Business travelers and tourists from many different countries stay at the hotel, and English is the most common language they communicate in. "Sometimes our guests need a tour guide, and, if I'm not too busy, I use the opportunity to practice my English." When he's not at work. Mr. Itani enjoys watching English-language TV. "It helps me a lot!" he says. Mr. Itani is married and has a one-year-old son.

Source: Authentic interviews of real people

A INFER INFORMATION Check all possible answers, according to the article.

1 Mr. Tanaka uses English . . .
☐ to teach classes.   ☐ to watch TV.
☐ with colleagues.   ☐ to use the Internet.

2 Ms. Marques uses English at work . . .
☐ in e-mails.   ☐ in international phone calls.
☐ in meetings.   ☐ in phone calls to other cities in Brazil.

3 Mr. Itani probably uses English with hotel guests from . . .
☐ Canada.   ☐ Lebanon.
☐ Brazil.   ☐ China.

B SCAN FOR FACTS Complete the information about the people.

	Mr. Tanaka	Ms. Marques	Mr. Itani
Occupation			
Lives in . . .			
Hometown			
Married?	☐yes ☐no	☐yes ☐no	☐yes ☐no

NOW YOU CAN Introduce someone to a group

A Read the information about each person. Then complete the two introductions.

Name: Victoria Wang
Nickname: Vicky
Occupation: photographer
Hometown: Wuhan, China
Birthplace: (same)
Age: 22
Favorite actor: Will Smith
Favorite sport: tennis
Other: lives in Shanghai

This is .... , but everyone calls her .... She's .... years old, and she's a .... Ms. .... lives in .... , but she is originally from a city called .... Her favorite actor is .... , and her favorite sport is ....

Name: Enrique Cruz
Nickname: Kiki
Occupation: pilot
Hometown: Veracruz, Mexico
Birthplace: Granada, Spain
Age: 41
Favorite actor: Matt Damon
Favorite sport: soccer
Other: lives in Monterrey, Mexico

Meet .... He's a .... , and he lives in .... Everyone calls him .... His hometown is .... , but actually he was born in .... His favorite actor is .... , and his favorite sport is .... Mr. Cruz is .... years old.

B NOTEPADDING Interview a classmate. Write his or her personal information on the notepad.

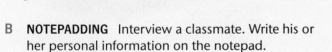

Name:
Nickname:
Occupation:
Hometown:
Birthplace:
Age:
Favorite actor:
Favorite sport:
Other:

C GROUP WORK Introduce your partner to your classmates. Use the introductions in Exercise A for support.

RECYCLE THIS LANGUAGE.

This is __.
I'd like you to meet __.
Everyone calls [him / her] __.
[His / Her] nickname is __.
[His / Her] hometown is __.
[His / Her] favorite __ is __.

Text-mining (optional)
Find and underline three words or phrases in the Reading that were new to you. Use them in your Group Work.
For example: "is originally from."

A ▶ 1:15 Listen to the conversations. Then listen again and write each person's occupation and nationality.

Australian   French
Brazilian   Polish

Name	Occupation	Nationality
1 George Detcheverry		
2 Sonia Pereira		
3 Mark Zaleski		
4 Marjorie Baxter		

B Complete each statement. Circle the correct word.

1 We're from (China / Chinese).

2 He's (Australia / Australian).

3 She's from (Italy / Italian).

4 My friend is (Uruguay / Uruguayan).

5 We're from (Japan / Japanese).

6 They're (Chile / Chilean).

7 My neighbors are from (Korea / Korean).

8 We're (Mexico / Mexican).

C Complete each conversation in your own way. (You don't need to give real information.)

1 "What city are you from?"
YOU ....

2 "What's your e-mail address?"
YOU ....

3 "Are you a teacher?"
YOU ....

4 YOU .... ?
"I'm from Canada."

5 YOU .... ?
"I'm a graphic designer."

6 YOU ....
"Great to meet you, too."

WRITING

Write a short description of the classmate you interviewed on page 11.
Include the following information.

- first and last name
- age
- occupation
- hometown
- birthplace
- favorite actor / sport

My partner's first name is Peter. His
last name is Hughes. He is twenty . . .

WRITING BOOSTER p. 142
- Capitalization
- Guidance for this writing exercise

For additional language practice . . .

♫ **TOP NOTCH** POP • Lyrics p. 149
"It's Nice to Meet You"

| DIGITAL SONG | DIGITAL KARAOKE |

ORAL REVIEW

CONTEST Form teams. Create questions for another team about Will Smith, using the verb <u>be</u>. (A team gets one point for each correct question and one point for each correct answer.) For example:

What's his nickname?

PAIR WORK

1 Create a conversation for the people in Picture 1. Start like this:

Who's Will Smith?

2 With a partner, invent personal information for the people in Picture 2. Then create a conversation.

Celebrity Screens
Web page of the rich and famous

Who is the real Will Smith?

Biography
real name: Willard Christopher Smith, Jr.
occupation: singer and actor
marital status: married
birth date: September 25, 1968
birthplace: Philadelphia, U.S.

Other information
favorite colors: red and black
favorite food: sweets
favorite actor: Harrison Ford

NOW I CAN

- ☐ Meet someone new.
- ☐ Identify and describe people.
- ☐ Provide personal information.
- ☐ Introduce someone to a group.

UNIT **2** Going Out

PREVIEW

COMMUNICATION GOALS
1 Accept or decline an invitation.
2 Express locations and give directions.
3 Make plans to see an event.
4 Talk about musical tastes.

Music ÷   My Tunes Store

Search Store

My Tunes **STORE**

GENRES
Rock / Pop
Hip-Hop
Jazz
Salsa
Rhythm & Blues
Classical
Movie Soundtracks
Folk
Show Tunes

DOWNLOADS
Albums
Singles / Songs
Music Videos

FEATURES
Share
Free MP3s

QUICK LINKS
Redeem
Support
My Alerts
My Account

Boomerang in Concert at Carnegie Hall
Rock / Pop

UPTOWN
Hip-Hop

Jazz Greats Volume 1: *Louis Armstrong / John Coltrane*
Jazz

LATIN DANCE PARTY SALSA 2016
Salsa

Loretta Walters *R&B for a Summer Night*
Rhythm & Blues

THE CHAPMAN QUARTET *All Beethoven Concert at Roxy Hall*
Classical

STAR NOW SHOWING Movie Magic Music from Your Favorite Films
Movie Soundtracks

FLUTES OF THE ANDES
Folk

A Pirate's Romance *A Musical Play by Roger Miller*
Show Tunes

A Do you download a lot of music from the Internet? Why or why not?

B ▶ 1:18 **VOCABULARY • Genres** Look at the web page. Then listen and repeat.

C **PAIR WORK** Which genres of music do you like? Are there genres that you hate? Tell your partner.

D **DISCUSSION** When you download music from the Internet, do you buy single songs or whole albums? Explain your answer.

E ▶ 1:19 **PHOTO STORY**   Read and listen to a conversation about music.

Meg: Hey. What's up?

Sara: Not much. Just downloading some new songs.

Meg: Downloading? That's not for me! Too much trouble! How about some live music tonight?

Sara: Sounds good. Where?

Meg: Klepto's playing at midnight at the Spot. Would you like to go?

Sara: At midnight? Sorry. That's past my bedtime.

Meg: Well, River T's there, too. They're playing at 8:00.

Sara: River T—the R & B group? Now that's more my style. I'm a real R & B fan.

Meg: Perfect! Meet you in front of the club at 7:45?

Sara: See you there!

F   **FOCUS ON LANGUAGE**   Find and write an underlined word or expression from the Photo Story with the same meaning:

1 That's too late for me. ....
2 Great! ....
3 music in a concert ....
4 What are you doing? ....
5 I like that better. ....
6 I don't like that. ....

G   **THINK AND EXPLAIN**   Choose an answer. Use a quotation to explain your answer.

1 What's Sara doing?
   a getting music from the Internet
   b buying tickets for a concert on the Internet

> 66 Sara says, 'Just downloading some new songs.' 99

2 What does Meg want to do?
   a download music from the Internet
   b go to a concert

3 Which woman doesn't like to go to sleep late?
   a Sara
   b Meg

4 When and where are they going to meet?
   a at midnight at River T
   b at the club before the show

SPEAKING

CLASS SURVEY   What kinds of music do you like? Number the genres in order, making number 1 your favorite. Then survey the class. Which are the most popular genres in your class?

.... classical music
.... folk music
.... hip-hop
.... movie soundtracks

.... jazz
.... R & B
.... rock / pop

.... salsa
.... show tunes
.... other

> 66 Who chose hip-hop as their favorite? 99

an electric guitar

GOAL Accept or decline an invitation

CONVERSATION MODEL

A ▶1:20 Read and listen to an invitation to a movie.

A: Are you free on Saturday? *The Pilots* is at the Movie Center. Would you like to go?

B: *The Pilots*? I'd love to go. What time?

A: At noon.

B: Great! See you there.

To decline . . .

B: Sorry. I'd love to go, but I'm busy on Saturday.

A: Too bad. Maybe some other time.

B ▶1:21 **RHYTHM AND INTONATION** Listen again and repeat. Then practice the Conversation Model with a partner.

GRAMMAR *Prepositions of time and place; Questions with* When, What time, *and* Where: *Review*

Prepositions of time

When's the concert? What time's the game? It's . . .

on	in	at
on Saturday	in March	at 8:30
on June 7th	in 2016	at midnight
on the 7th	in the summer	at noon
on Monday, May 3rd	in the morning	
on Tuesday morning	in ten minutes	

Prepositions of place

Where's the movie? It's . . .

on	in	at
on Fifth Avenue	in Mexico	at the Film Forum
on the corner	in Tokyo	at work
on the street	in the park	at school
on the left	in the neighborhood	at the art gallery

Contractions

When's = When is
What time's = What time is
Where's = Where is

Be careful!

Don't contract are with When, What time, or Where.
Where are your parents?
NOT ~~Where're~~ your parents?

GRAMMAR BOOSTER p. 125
- Prepositions of time and place: usage rules
- Would like for preference: review and expansion

GRAMMAR PRACTICE Complete the message with prepositions of time and place.

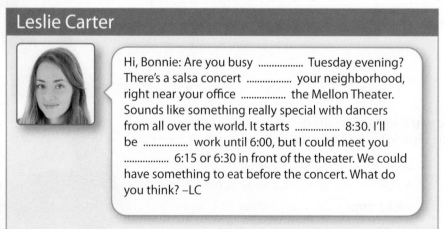

Leslie Carter

Hi, Bonnie: Are you busy .... Tuesday evening? There's a salsa concert .... your neighborhood, right near your office .... the Mellon Theater. Sounds like something really special with dancers from all over the world. It starts .... 8:30. I'll be .... work until 6:00, but I could meet you .... 6:15 or 6:30 in front of the theater. We could have something to eat before the concert. What do you think? –LC

VOCABULARY *Entertainment and cultural events*

A ▶1:22 Read and listen. Then listen again and repeat.

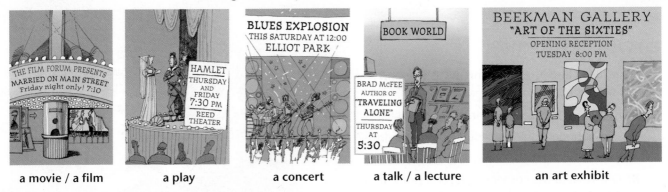

a movie / a film   a play   a concert   a talk / a lecture   an art exhibit

B **PAIR WORK** Ask and answer questions about the events in the pictures above. Use <u>When</u>, <u>Where</u>, and <u>What time</u>.

❝ Where's the talk? ❞

❝ It's at Book World. ❞

C ▶1:23 **LISTEN FOR DETAILS** Listen to the conversations. Match the event and the place.

.... **1** *Agamemnon*   **a** at the Cinema Center

.... **2** the Boston Symphony Orchestra   **b** at the City Nights Bookstore

.... **3** *Bus Stop*   **c** at the Theater in the Circle

.... **4** Nick Hornby   **d** at the Festival

D ▶1:24 **LISTEN TO DRAW CONCLUSIONS** Listen to the conversations again. Complete the chart.

	Kind of event	**Time of event**	**Does the person want to go?** (Write <u>yes</u>, <u>no</u>, or <u>maybe</u>.)
1			
2			
3			
4			

NOW YOU CAN Accept or decline an invitation

A **CONVERSATION ACTIVATOR** With a partner, change the Conversation Model. Use these events or other events. Decide to accept or decline. Then change roles.

A: Are you free .... ? .... at ....
Would you like to go?

B: .... I'd love to go. ....

DON'T STOP!
If you decline, suggest a different event.

RECYCLE THIS LANGUAGE.
Sounds good.
Great!
Perfect!
That's past my bedtime.
That's not for me.
That's more my style.
Well, how about __?
See you there!

This week's Entertainment

MOVIES — *Red Sunset* The Cine Lux, Sat./Sun. 8:55 P.M.

MUSIC — *The Soul Brothers* The Supermarket, Fri. Midnight

TALKS — *John Grisham, writer* Book Town, Mon. 8:00 P.M.

PLAYS — *Romeo and Juliet* The Bridge Theater, Every night 7:30 P.M.

B **CHANGE PARTNERS** Practice the conversation again. Use different events.

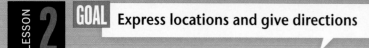
CONVERSATION MODEL

A ▶1:25 Read and listen to someone ask for and get directions.

A: Excuse me. I'm looking for the National Bank.

B: The National Bank? Do you know the address?

A: Yes. It's 205 Holly Avenue.

B: Oh. Walk to the corner of First and Holly. It's right around the corner, across from the museum.

A: Thank you!

Or if you don't know . . .

B: The National Bank? I'm sorry. I'm not from around here.

A: Thanks, anyway.

B ▶1:26 **RHYTHM AND INTONATION** Listen again and repeat. Then practice the Conversation Model with a partner.

DIGITAL FLASH CARDS
VOCABULARY *Locations and directions*

A ▶1:27 Read and listen. Then listen again and repeat.

Locations	Where is (the) _____ ?

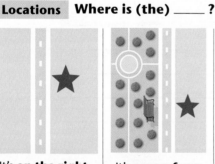
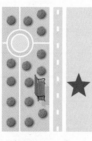

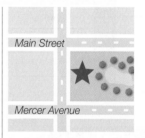

It's **on the right side** of the street.	It's **across from** the park.	It's **down the street from** the museum.	It's **around the corner from** the theater.	It's **between** Main (Street) **and** Mercer (Avenue).

Directions	How do I get to (the) _____ ?

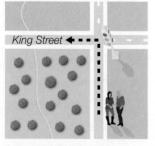
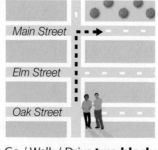
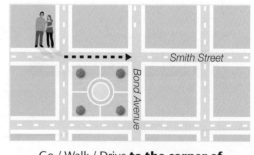

Turn left at the corner / **at** the light / **on** King Street.	Go / Walk / Drive **two blocks and turn right**.	Go / Walk / Drive **to the corner of** Smith (Street) **and** Bond (Avenue).

B ▶1:28 **LISTEN FOR LOCATIONS** Listen to the conversations about places. Write the number of each place in a box on the map. (Be careful: There are three places but seven boxes.)

C **PAIR WORK** Use the Vocabulary from page 18 to tell your partner where you live.

> " My house is on Grove Street between Dodd Street and Park Street. "

OCEAN CITY

PRONUNCIATION *Rising intonation to confirm information*

A ▶1:29 Repeat information with rising intonation to be sure you understand. Read and listen. Then listen again and repeat.

1 A: Where's the library?
   B: The library?↗

2 A: Let's meet at the mall.
   B: The mall?↗

B **PAIR WORK** Talk about two other places. Practice confirming information with rising intonation.

NOW YOU CAN Express locations and give directions

A **CONVERSATION ACTIVATOR** Use the Vocabulary and the Piermont map (or a map of your own town or neighborhood) to change the Conversation Model. Then change roles.

A: Excuse me. I'm looking for ....
B: .... ? Do you know the address?
A: Yes. It's ....
B: Oh. ....

DON'T STOP!
Ask about other locations.

Book World

CLARK STREET

The Dance Palace

83

85

SECOND AVENUE

HOLLY AVENUE

The National Bank

The Film Forum

First Avenue Coffee House

You are here.

121

205

127

204

FIRST AVENUE

HARPER STREET

101

The Bell Theater

128

126

The Piermont Museum of Art

Mr. Bean Coffee Shop

The Taft Symphony Hall

B **CHANGE PARTNERS** Ask about other locations and give directions.

BEFORE YOU LISTEN

PREVIEW Look at the tickets below. Name two kinds of events you can go to at the Kingston Culturefest.

LISTENING COMPREHENSION

A ▶1:30 **LISTEN FOR DETAILS** Listen to people calling the Kingston Culturefest. Look at the tickets. Then listen again and complete the information in the boxes.

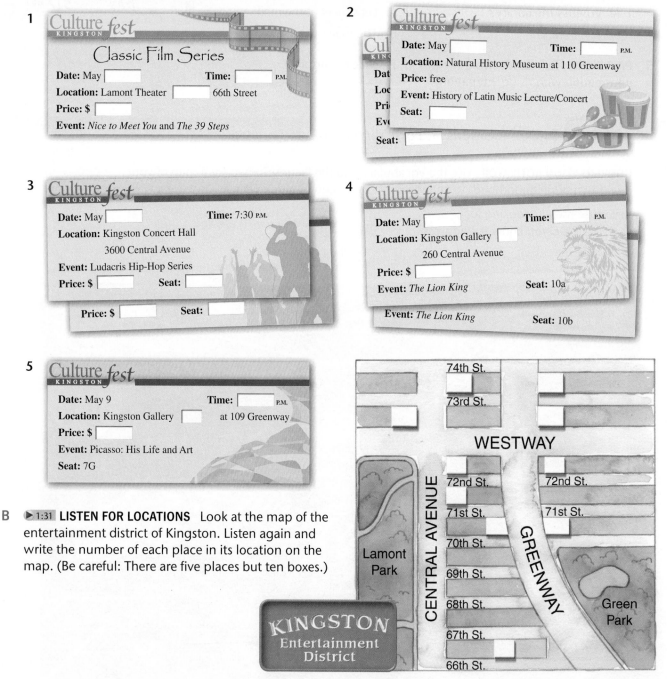

1

Culture *fest*
KINGSTON

Classic Film Series

Date: May [ ] **Time:** [ ] P.M.
Location: Lamont Theater [ ] 66th Street
Price: $ [ ]
Event: *Nice to Meet You* and *The 39 Steps*

2

Culture *fest*
KINGSTON

Date: May [ ] **Time:** [ ] P.M.
Location: Natural History Museum at 110 Greenway
Price: free
Event: History of Latin Music Lecture/Concert
Seat: [ ]

Seat: [ ]

3

Culture *fest*
KINGSTON

Date: May [ ] **Time:** 7:30 P.M.
Location: Kingston Concert Hall
3600 Central Avenue
Event: Ludacris Hip-Hop Series
Price: $ [ ] **Seat:** [ ]

Price: $ [ ] **Seat:** [ ]

4

Culture *fest*
KINGSTON

Date: May [ ] **Time:** [ ] P.M.
Location: Kingston Gallery [ ]
260 Central Avenue
Price: $ [ ]
Event: *The Lion King* **Seat:** 10a

Event: *The Lion King* **Seat:** 10b

5

Culture *fest*
KINGSTON

Date: May 9 **Time:** [ ] P.M.
Location: Kingston Gallery [ ] at 109 Greenway
Price: $ [ ]
Event: Picasso: His Life and Art
Seat: 7G

B ▶1:31 **LISTEN FOR LOCATIONS** Look at the map of the entertainment district of Kingston. Listen again and write the number of each place in its location on the map. (Be careful: There are five places but ten boxes.)

A **NOTEPADDING** Read about all the events for the week of May 6–12 below and on the tickets on page 20. Choose events you want to see. Write those events, times, and places on the notepad.

Event	Day / Date / Time	Place

Kingston Post

THIS WEEK at the **KINGSTON** *Culture* fest

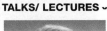

| MON 6 | TUES 7 | WED 8 | THURS 9 | FRI 10 | SAT 11 | SUN 12 |

HIGHLIGHTS

FILM

Brother and sister directors **Fumiko** and **Daiki** Ito introduce their movie *Hip-Hop High School*, this year's International Teen Oscar winner for Best Movie.

Monday and Thursday
7:45 P.M.

Kingston Gallery 2

Member price: $5
General admission: $12
Special teen price: $5

THEATER

Andrew Lloyd Weber's classical musical

Cats

Lamont Theater

Tuesday to Friday 8:00 P.M.

Tkts: **Balcony** from $65
Orchestra from $85

" *A Serious Play For Serious Theatergoers* "

The Dentist's Chair

Kingston Gallery 2

Friday and Saturday 8:00 P.M.

CONCERTS

Joshua Bell, Violinist.

Bell will play Estrellita by Manuel María Ponce and Stravinsky's The Rite of Spring with the Mexico City Philharmonic Orchestra.

Kingston Concert Hall

Wednesday and Saturday: 8:00 P.M.

Sunday: 2:00 P.M. (matinee)
Tkts: $50 (students $25)

Bruno Mars

Singer songwriter Bruno Mars sings from his favorite album Earth to Mars, featuring "Just the Way You Are."

Kingston Gallery 2

Tuesday, Wednesday, and Friday 10:00 P.M. / late show: 12:30 A.M.
Tkts: $23

TALKS/ LECTURES

Reinvent a Better World

Melinda Gates (of the Bill and Melinda Gates Foundation)

Tuesday 6:30 P.M. and 9:00 P.M.

Natural History Museum

Free!

B **PAIR WORK** Compare the events you want to see. Make plans to see one or more of the events together. Use the map on page 20.

RECYCLE THIS LANGUAGE.

Invite
Are you free / busy on __?
There's a [play] at __.
Would you like to go?

Ask for information
How about __?
What time's the __?
Where is the __?

Accept and decline
I'd love to go.
I'm a real __ fan.
See you at __.
I'd love to go, but __.
Maybe some other time.
That's past my bedtime.
I'm [not] a __ fan.
That's not for me.
That's more my style.

Locations / Directions
It's across from the __.
It's around the corner from the __.
It's on the __ side of the street.
It's between __ and __.
Turn left at __.
Go / Walk / Drive to __.

BEFORE YOU READ

WARM-UP In what ways is music important to you?

READING ▶1:32

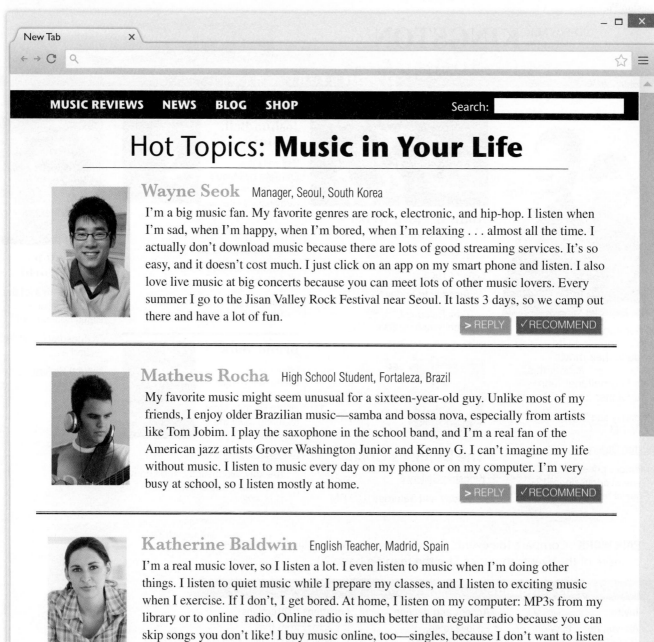

MUSIC REVIEWS   NEWS   BLOG   SHOP   Search:

Hot Topics: **Music in Your Life**

Wayne Seok Manager, Seoul, South Korea

I'm a big music fan. My favorite genres are rock, electronic, and hip-hop. I listen when I'm sad, when I'm happy, when I'm bored, when I'm relaxing . . . almost all the time. I actually don't download music because there are lots of good streaming services. It's so easy, and it doesn't cost much. I just click on an app on my smart phone and listen. I also love live music at big concerts because you can meet lots of other music lovers. Every summer I go to the Jisan Valley Rock Festival near Seoul. It lasts 3 days, so we camp out there and have a lot of fun.

> REPLY   ✓RECOMMEND

Matheus Rocha High School Student, Fortaleza, Brazil

My favorite music might seem unusual for a sixteen-year-old guy. Unlike most of my friends, I enjoy older Brazilian music—samba and bossa nova, especially from artists like Tom Jobim. I play the saxophone in the school band, and I'm a real fan of the American jazz artists Grover Washington Junior and Kenny G. I can't imagine my life without music. I listen to music every day on my phone or on my computer. I'm very busy at school, so I listen mostly at home.

> REPLY   ✓RECOMMEND

Katherine Baldwin English Teacher, Madrid, Spain

I'm a real music lover, so I listen a lot. I even listen to music when I'm doing other things. I listen to quiet music while I prepare my classes, and I listen to exciting music when I exercise. If I don't, I get bored. At home, I listen on my computer: MP3s from my library or to online radio. Online radio is much better than regular radio because you can skip songs you don't like! I buy music online, too—singles, because I don't want to listen to 12 songs in a row by the same musician. You know what I hate? Big concerts in an arena where you can't see the musicians. I prefer shows in small clubs.

> REPLY   ✓RECOMMEND

Source: Authentic interviews of real people

A **CONFIRM CONTENT** Read the following statements. Circle T (<u>true</u>), F (<u>false</u>), or NI (<u>no information</u>) for each, based on information in the Reading. Explain your answer.

T F NI **1** Wayne Seok is a fan of live music.

T F NI **2** He doesn't like folk music.

T F NI **3** Matheus Rocha usually listens to music on CDs.

T F NI **4** His friends all like samba and bossa nova.

T F NI **5** Katherine Baldwin doesn't like big concerts.

T F NI **6** She likes music videos.

B **MAKE PERSONAL COMPARISONS** Who are you like: Mr. Seok, Mr. Rocha, or Ms. Baldwin? Explain how.

> " I'm like Ms. Baldwin. I listen to music while I do other things. "

NOW YOU CAN **Talk about musical tastes**

A **FRAME YOUR IDEAS** Fill out the survey about your musical tastes.

MUSIC IN YOUR LIFE   Take the Survey

1. Are you a music fan? ☐ yes ☐ no

2. What's your favorite kind of music?
☐ rock / pop   ☐ classical   ☐ movie soundtracks
☐ jazz   ☐ hip-hop   ☐ salsa
☐ folk   ☐ show tunes   ☐ R & B
☐ other _____

3. Who are your favorite singers? _____
musicians? _____
groups? _____

4. When do you listen to music?
☐ when I study   ☐ when I exercise   ☐ when I relax
☐ when I'm happy   ☐ when I'm bored   ☐ when I'm sad
☐ when I drive   ☐ all the time   ☐ when I work
☐ other _____

5. Do you go to concerts?
☐ often   ☐ sometimes   ☐ never
If so, what's your favorite kind of concert?
_____

6. How do you listen to music?
☐ on CDs   ☐ on the Internet
☐ on the radio   ☐ on music videos
☐ on MP3s   ☐ on TV music channels
☐ on my phone   ☐ other _____

7. How many songs are in your library? _____
How many albums? _____
What kinds of music? _____

B **PAIR WORK** Compare surveys with a partner. Summarize your answers on the notepad.

About me	About my partner
I'm a hip-hop fan.	Her favorite music is hip-hop, too.

C **DISCUSSION** Now use the notepad to tell the class about your musical tastes.

> " My partner and I love music. We're real hip-hop fans! "

Text-mining (optional)
Find and underline three words or phrases in the Reading that were new to you. Use them in your Discussion.
For example: "I'm a big music fan."

REVIEW

A ▶1:33 Listen to the conversations about entertainment and cultural events. Complete the chart with the kind of event and the time of the event.

	Kind of event	Time of event
1		
2		
3		

B ▶1:34 Look at the chart and listen again. Circle the event if the person accepts the invitation.

C Complete each conversation, based on the picture.

1
A: There's a great .... at the City Theater.
B: .... 's the show?
A: Eight o'clock.

2
A: I'm sorry I'm late. This .... is awesome. What time did it start?
B: .... 6:30. Don't worry. You didn't miss much.

3
A: Hello?
B: Hi. Are you busy? I'm at the Beekman Gallery. There's an .... of paintings from France.
A: Sounds great! Meet you there .... fifteen minutes?

4
A: Are you free .... Monday evening? Dr. Benson is giving a .... on the native plants of the desert. Do you want to go?
B: That depends. .... time?
A: It's .... 7:00.

D Unscramble the sentences. Then match the sentences with the pictures. Write the number on the picture.

1 on / Martine Avenue / The bookstore / is / the corner of / and Bank Street
....

2 8:00 P.M. / Saturday, / The exhibit is / on / August 3 / at
....

3 around / the street / The movie theater / is / the corner / and / down
....

4 the corner / The house / is / around / the street / and across
....

WRITING

Write at least five sentences about yourself and your tastes in music.

> My name is Kazu Sato. I'm from Nagoya. I'm a
> classical music fan. I love Mozart . . .

WRITING BOOSTER p. 142
• The sentence
• Guidance for this writing exercise

For additional language practice . . .

♫ TOP NOTCH POP • Lyrics p. 149
"Going Out"

DIGITAL SONG   DIGITAL KARAOKE

ORAL REVIEW

CONTEST Form teams. Study the ads for one minute. Then close your books. With your team, name all the events you can remember. (Your team gets one point for each correct event.)

PAIR WORK Create conversations for the two people.

1 Ask and answer questions about the ads. Use <u>When</u>, <u>What time</u>, and <u>Where</u>. For example:

Q: *Where's the lecture?*
A: *It's . . .*

2 Discuss the ads. Make plans, suggestions, and invitations. Discuss your likes and dislikes.

The Journal News- October 22

Today's Entertainment

B16

MOVIES

The House
on the Other Side of the Street

"AWESOME . . . YOU WON'T SLEEP FOR A WEEK" - Newstime
"Don't bring the kids." - Theodore Roper

PLAZA THEATER
237-FILM 10:25 P.M. 1:00 A.M.

In a world where anything could happen, at any time . . .

DO YOU HAVE ANY WATER IN THAT BOTTLE?

" A hilarious spoof of airport culture"
Alizia Compton, *Today's Arts Magazine*

Do You Have Any Liquids?

Mama Cruz   Rachel Weldon

CinePlex 2
5:25, 7:05, 9:30

PLAYS

Wicked
Hill Street Theater
660 North Main
8:30 P.M.

MUSIC

Nora Jones
singer / songwriter

TODAY ONLY
City Limits Jazz Club
9:30 P.M.

The China Philharmonic Orchestra with The Shanghai Opera House Chorus
Mozart's Requiem
Symphony Hall, 8:00 P.M.

OTHER EVENTS - Talks/Lectures
James M Cowan
A Plan for Everyday Life
Lecture, discussion, book signing
Books and Other Precious Things
400 Jackson Street   6:45 P.M.

NOW I CAN

☐ Accept or decline an invitation.
☐ Express locations and give directions.
☐ Make plans to see an event.
☐ Talk about musical tastes.

UNIT 3 The Extended Family

COMMUNICATION GOALS

1 Report news about relationships.
2 Describe extended families.
3 Compare people.
4 Discuss family cultural traditions.

PREVIEW

I'm Andrew. This is **my wife**, Diane. And this is my family.

grandparents

my **grandmother**   my **grandfather**

Tina   Daniel

parents   in-laws

my **uncle**   my **aunt**   my ....   my ....   my **mother-in-law**   my **father-in-law**

Nick   Gina

Trey   Amy
my **cousins**   Barbara   Rick   Louise   Tom

my **sister-in-law**   my ....   my ....   my **brother-in-law**

Maureen   Jeff

Ellen   Seth   Carrie   Zach   Jenny
children   David

my **niece**   my **nephew**   my ....   my ....

A FAMILY VOCABULARY REVIEW Look at Andrew's family photos. Write the six missing relationship words.

B ▶2:02 VOCABULARY • The Extended Family Listen and repeat.

C PAIR WORK Ask and answer questions about Andrew's relatives. Use Who.

❝ Who are Barbara and Rick? ❞

❝ They're Diane's in-laws. ❞

❝ Who's Jeff's wife? ❞

❝ Maureen. ❞

D ▶ 2:03 **PHOTO STORY**   Read and listen to two women discussing family photos.

Emma: Who's that guy? Your brother?

Grace: No, that's my brother-in-law, Matthew. He's married to my older sister, Alexa. And this is their son, Aiden. He's adopted.*

Emma: Do they have any other children?

Grace: No, just the one. He's an only child.

Emma: Looks like they're having a great time in New York.

Grace: Actually, they live there.

Emma: They do? Wow! How often do you see them?

Grace: We get together about twice a year.

Emma: And what about these kids?

Grace: They're my younger sister's. Ariana's the girl. And these are her little brothers, Cole and Casey.

Emma: Cole and Casey look so much alike! Are they twins?*

Grace: They are. They all live in Vancouver, but we keep in touch on the Internet.

*adopted: Matthew and Alexa aren't Aiden's birth parents.

*twins: Cole and Casey were born at the same time.

E   **THINK AND EXPLAIN**   Check <u>true</u> or <u>false</u>, based on information from the Photo Story. Then explain each answer.

	true	false
1 Grace is Aiden's aunt.	☐	☐
2 Grace is Matthew's sister-in-law.	☐	☐
3 Matthew is Ariana's brother-in-law.	☐	☐
4 Alexa has one niece and three nephews.	☐	☐
5 Ariana, Cole, and Casey are Aiden's cousins.	☐	☐
6 Matthew and Alexa have two children.	☐	☐

❝ It's true. Aiden is her sister's son. ❞

SPEAKING

A   Complete the chart with information about your extended family. Write the number of people for each relationship.

I have . . .		
.... brother(s)	.... uncle(s)	.... cousin(s)
.... sister(s)	.... aunt(s)	.... brother(s)-in-law
.... nephew(s)	.... niece(s)	.... sister(s)-in-law

B   **GROUP WORK**   Compare charts with your classmates. Who in your class has a very large extended family?

❝ How many ____s do you have? ❞

GOAL Report news about relationships

VOCABULARY *Relationships and marital status*

A ▶2:04 Read and listen. Then listen again and repeat.

They're **single**.

They're **engaged**.
(He's her **fiancé**. / She's his **fiancée**.)

They're **married**.

They're **separated**.

They're **divorced**.
(He's her **ex-husband**. / She's his **ex-wife**.)

She's **widowed**.

B ▶2:05 **LISTEN TO CLASSIFY** Listen and infer the marital status of the person in each conversation. Circle the correct status.

1 The woman is (single / engaged / married).

2 His aunt is (engaged / widowed / divorced).

3 His sister is (engaged / separated / divorced).

4 Her sister is (engaged / separated / divorced).

GRAMMAR *The simple present tense: Review*

Affirmative statements

My in-laws **live** in Rio.
My ex-wife **lives** in Tokyo.

Negative statements

My aunt and uncle **don't work** in an office.
My cousin **doesn't work** at home.

Contractions
don't = do not
doesn't = does not

Yes / no questions and short answers

Do they **have** any children? Yes, they do. / No, they don't.
Does she **have** any nieces or nephews? Yes, she does. / No, she doesn't.

Spelling rules with <u>he</u>, <u>she</u>, and <u>it</u>

Add <u>-s</u> to the base form of most verbs.
  works likes plays calls

Add <u>-es</u> to verbs that end in <u>-s</u>, <u>-sh</u>, <u>-ch</u>, or <u>-x</u>.
  washes watches relaxes

Exceptions:
  do → does
  go → goes
  have → has
  study → studies

GRAMMAR BOOSTER p. 126
• The simple present tense: usage and form

GRAMMAR PRACTICE   Complete the conversations. Use the simple present tense.

1 A: .... your cousin .... (have) any children?

   B: Yes, she .... She .... two kids—a girl and a boy.

2 A: .... your in-laws .... (live) in Toronto?

   B: No, they .... They .... in Ottawa.

3 A: .... your parents .... (work) in Quito?

   B: Yes, they .... They .... for the government.

4 A: .... your fiancé .... (like) hip-hop?

   B: No, he .... He .... it at all.

5 A: .... her ex-husband .... (see) their kids?

   B: Yes, he .... He .... them a lot.

6 A: .... you .... (call) your nieces every day?

   B: No, I .... They .... *me*!

CONVERSATION MODEL

A ▶2:06 Read and listen to good news about a relationship.

   A: What's new?

   B: Actually, I have some good news. My sister just got engaged!

   A: That's great. Congratulations!

   B: Thanks!

   A: So tell me about her fiancé. What does he do?

   B: Well, he works at Redcor. He's an engineer.

   Or bad news . . .

   B: Actually, I have some bad news. My sister just got divorced.

   A: I'm sorry to hear that. Is she OK?

   B: Yes, she is. Thanks for asking.

B ▶2:07 **RHYTHM AND INTONATION**   Listen again and repeat. Then practice the Conversation Model with a partner.

NOW YOU CAN   Report news about relationships

A **NOTEPADDING**   Imagine that you have good or bad news about someone in your extended family (or use real news). Write notes to plan a conversation.

B **CONVERSATION ACTIVATOR**   Personalize the Conversation Model. Tell your partner your news. Then change roles.

   A: What's new?

   B: Actually, I have some .... news. My ....

   A: ....

C **CHANGE PARTNERS**   Practice the conversation again. Report other good or bad news.

Relationship to you:
What's the news?
What does he / she do?
Other information:

DON'T STOP!

Ask yes / no questions.
Is [she] ___? / Does [he] ___? / Do [they] ___?

Use the simple present tense to say more.
He lives / works ___.
She likes / hates / studies ___.
They have / don't have ___.

good news
got married
got engaged

bad news
got separated
got divorced

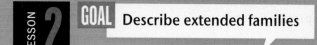

LESSON 2 · GOAL Describe extended families

VOCABULARY *Other family relationships*

A ▶2:08 Read and listen. Then listen again and repeat.

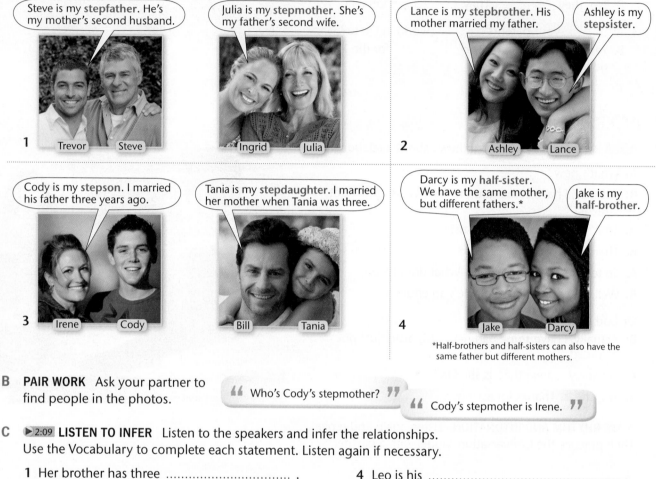

Steve is my **stepfather**. He's my mother's second husband.

1 · Trevor · Steve

Julia is my **stepmother**. She's my father's second wife.

Ingrid · Julia

Lance is my **stepbrother**. His mother married my father.

Ashley is my **stepsister**.

2 · Ashley · Lance

Cody is my **stepson**. I married his father three years ago.

3 · Irene · Cody

Tania is my **stepdaughter**. I married her mother when Tania was three.

Bill · Tania

Darcy is my **half-sister**. We have the same mother, but different fathers.*

Jake is my **half-brother**.

4 · Jake · Darcy

*Half-brothers and half-sisters can also have the same father but different mothers.

B **PAIR WORK** Ask your partner to find people in the photos.

❝ Who's Cody's stepmother? ❞

❝ Cody's stepmother is Irene. ❞

C ▶2:09 **LISTEN TO INFER** Listen to the speakers and infer the relationships. Use the Vocabulary to complete each statement. Listen again if necessary.

1 Her brother has three ....

2 Carol is his ....

3 She calls her .... "Mom."

4 Leo is his ....

5 Hank is her ....

GRAMMAR *The simple present tense—information questions: Review*

What **do** your in-laws **do**?	What **does** your sister-in-law **do**?
Where **do** their cousins **live**?	Where **does** your stepsister **live**?
When **do** you **visit** your aunt?	When **does** your brother **visit** his niece?
Who **do** their stepchildren **live** with?	Who **does** your stepdaughter **live** with?
How often **do** you **call** your niece?	How often **does** she **call** her nephew?
How many children **do** they **have**?	How many half-brothers **does** he **have**?

Be careful! <u>Who</u> as subject:
Who **lives** in Hong Kong?
NOT Who ~~does live~~ in Hong Kong?

GRAMMAR BOOSTER p. 127
Information questions in the simple present tense:
• Form
• Questions with <u>Who</u>
• Common errors

A **FIND THE GRAMMAR** Look at the Photo Story on page 27 again. Find and underline one information question in the simple present tense.

B GRAMMAR PRACTICE Complete the conversations with the simple present tense.

1 A: .... your sister .... ?
   B: She lives in Dublin.

2 A: .... nieces and nephews .... ?
   B: Three. My sister .... two girls—both adopted—and my brother .... a stepson.

3 A: .... stay with when you visit Los Angeles?
   B: I .... with my aunt and uncle.

4 A: .... with your grandfather?
   B: My half-sister Louise lives with him.

5 A: .... your stepfather do?
   B: He .... in a restaurant. He's the chef and manager.

6 A: .... your uncle work?
   B: At the hospital around the corner.
   A: .... your aunt .... there, too?
   B: No, ...

CONVERSATION MODEL

A ▶2:10 Read and listen to people describing their families.

   A: Do you come from a large family?

   B: Not really. I have two brothers.

   A: What about aunts and uncles?

   B: Well, I have three aunts on my father's side. And on my mother's side, I have two aunts and three uncles.

   A: That's pretty big!

B ▶2:11 **RHYTHM AND INTONATION** Listen again and repeat. Then practice the Conversation Model with a partner.

NOW YOU CAN Describe extended families

A **NOTEPADDING** List your extended family relationships on the notepad.

B **CONVERSATION ACTIVATOR** With a partner, use your notepads to personalize the Conversation Model. Describe your extended family. Then change roles.

   A: Do you come from a large family?
   B: .... I have ....
   A: What about .... ?
   B: Well, I have .... on my .... 's side. And ....
   A: ....

On my father's side . . .	On my mother's side . . .

DON'T STOP!

Ask for more information.
Tell me about your [aunts / uncles / cousins].
What about your [sister-in-law]?
Does he ___? / Do they ___?
Is she / Are they [single]?

What ___?   How old ___?
Where ___?   How often ___?
When ___?   How many ___?
Who ___?

C **GROUP WORK** Now tell your classmates about your partner's extended family.

GOAL Compare people

BEFORE YOU LISTEN

A ▶2:12 **VOCABULARY** • *Similarities and differences*
Read and listen. Then listen again and repeat.

How are you similar?

We **look alike**.

We wear **the same kind of** clothes.

We **both** like rock music.

How are you different?

We **look different**.

We wear **different kinds of** clothes.

I like rock, **but** he likes classical.

B **PAIR WORK** Find similarities and differences between you and a partner. Write sentences describing the similarities and differences. Use the Vocabulary.

LISTENING COMPREHENSION

A ▶2:13 **LISTEN TO IDENTIFY SIMILARITIES AND DIFFERENCES** Listen to Lucille talk about herself and her sister, Laura. Check the statements that are true. Explain your answers.

Lucille and Laura . . .		
1	☐ look alike.	☐ look different.
2	☐ like the same kind of food.	☐ like different kinds of food.
3	☐ like the same kind of movies.	☐ like different kinds of movies.
4	☐ like the same kind of music.	☐ like different kinds of music.
5	☐ have the same number of kids.	☐ have different numbers of kids.
6	Lucille and Laura are ☐ twins. ☐ stepsisters. ☐ half-sisters.	

B ▶2:14 **LISTEN TO TAKE NOTES** Listen again for what Lucille says about these topics. On your notepad, use the Vocabulary to write sentences about how she and her sister are similar or different.

appearance	*Lucille and Laura look alike.*	favorite colors	
sports preferences		musical tastes	
families		clothes	

appearance *Lucille and Laura look alike.*	favorite colors
sports preferences	musical tastes
families	clothes

PRONUNCIATION *Linking sounds*

A ▶2:15 Read and listen. Pay attention to the linking of sounds in <u>does she</u> and <u>does he</u>. Then listen again and repeat.

/dʌʃi/
1 Does she have any stepchildren?

/dʌzi/
3 Does he live near you?

/dʌʃi/
2 How many stepchildren does she have?

/dʌzi/
4 Where does he live?

B Now practice the questions on your own. Pay attention to blended sounds.

NOW YOU CAN Compare people

A **NOTEPADDING** Choose someone in your extended family. On the notepad, write your similarities and differences. Use the Vocabulary from page 32.

The person's name:	Relationship to you:
	You Both of you Your relative

Ideas
- marital status
- occupation
- family relationships
- appearance
- clothing
- likes and dislikes
- abilities

B **PAIR WORK** Tell your partner about you and your relative. Use your notepad. Then compare other people in your families.

RECYCLE THIS LANGUAGE.

Similarities and differences
How are you similar?
How are you different?
Do you look alike?
Do you both __?
Do you __ the same kind of __?
Do you __ different kinds of __?

For more information
How about __?
Do you have any __?
How old __?
What does your __ do?
Where does your __ live?
How many __ does your __ have?

❝ My cousin and I are both single. ❞

❝ My uncle likes rock music, but my aunt likes classical. ❞

GOAL Discuss family cultural traditions

BEFORE YOU READ

WARM-UP In your opinion, how long should adult children live in their parents' homes?

READING ▶ 2:16

Ask Mr. Dad ✕ ＋

← | → ↻ ☆ http: www.mrdad.com ▶

Ask Mr. Dad With Armin Brott

| Home | About Mr. Dad | Get Advice | Mr. Dad Blog | Reviews |

When Adult Children Come Home

Do you have a question?
Ask Mr. Dad

Q: *My wife and I recently sent our last child off to college. We are ready to sell the house and travel, but our oldest daughter doesn't have a job and plans to move back home. What should we do?*

A: Most North Americans expect their children to move out of the house at eighteen. But that's changing. Today, more adult children are returning home to live. Some don't have jobs or can't pay for the high costs of housing. Some are recently separated or divorced. Most are single, but some come home with a wife, husband, or child, too.

Most parents are happy when their kids come back home to live. However, when a son or daughter can't find a job—or is recently divorced—there can be problems. And if their son or daughter is still at home at the age of thirty-five, many parents are no longer happy.

In your case, what if your daughter moves back home?

- Don't worry. If you and your daughter had a good relationship when she was younger, she'll be fine. Help her in any way you can. And it's OK to ask, "How long do you plan on staying?"

- Don't treat your daughter like a child. In our culture, adult children don't feel good about living at home, and they don't want to depend on their parents' help. Tell her you understand.

- Talk to your daughter as an adult. Have a discussion about paying for expenses and helping with household responsibilities and chores, such as kitchen cleanup and doing laundry. If you and your daughter talk and try to understand each other, everyone will be happier.

Source: www.mrdad.com

A **CONFIRM FACTS** Complete each statement.

1 The parents are worried because their daughter ....
   a wants to move into their home
   b wants to move away from their home
   c doesn't want to leave their home
   d doesn't want to come home

2 According to Armin Brott, most North Americans expect children to move out of their parents' home when they ....
   a reach the age of eighteen
   b finish college
   c find a job
   d get married

B INFER INFORMATION Check all the correct answers, according to what Armin Brott says.

1 What are the reasons adult children are moving back home?
- ☐ They don't have jobs.
- ☐ They get divorced.
- ☐ They can't afford housing.
- ☐ They feel good about living with their parents.
- ☐ They want to depend on their parents.

2 What are Mr. Brott's suggestions to the father?
- ☐ to sell his house and go traveling
- ☐ to discuss chores at home
- ☐ to ask his daughter to find a job
- ☐ to try to understand his daughter
- ☐ to not worry too much about his daughter

DIGITAL MORE EXERCISES

NOW YOU CAN Discuss family cultural traditions

A FRAME YOUR IDEAS Complete the survey about adult children in your country. Then compare answers with a partner.

Living At Home?

1 At what age do children usually leave home in your country?
- ☐ between 18 and 20
- ☐ between 21 and 25
- ☐ between 26 and 30
- ☐ over 30
- ☐ It depends on their marital status.

2 What are the reasons adult children usually leave home?
- ☐ They get a job.
- ☐ They get married.
- ☐ They go away to study.
- ☐ They don't want to depend on their parents.
- ☐ Other ....

3 How do parents feel when their adult children are living at home?
- ☐ They're very happy.
- ☐ They're very worried.
- ☐ They don't think about it.
- ☐ They don't want them to stay.
- ☐ Other ....

4 What do adult children usually do when they live at home?
- ☐ They help with the chores.
- ☐ They help pay for expenses.
- ☐ They look for a job.
- ☐ They look for a new place to live.
- ☐ Other ....

B NOTEPADDING Write some similarities and differences between family cultural traditions in your country and those Armin Brott describes.

What's the same?	What's different?

C GROUP WORK Imagine you are speaking to a visitor to your country. Explain your country's family cultural traditions about adult children living at home. Use your notepad.

Text-mining (optional)
Find and underline three words or phrases in the Reading that were new to you. Use them in your Group Work. For example: "household responsibilities."

A ▶2:17 Listen to the people talk about their families. Check the box for family size for each speaker. Then listen again and write the number of children in each person's family.

		A big family	A small family	Number of children
1	Brenda	☐	☐	
2	Steven	☐	☐	
3	Leslie	☐	☐	
4	Jason	☐	☐	

B Complete the sentences with the correct word or phrase.

   1 Larry doesn't have any brothers or sisters. He's an ....

   2 Bob's brother is Ron. They have the same birth date. They are ....

   3 Jun's brother has two daughters. They are Jun's ....

   4 Eva is Alfonso's wife. Alfonso's parents are Eva's ....

   5 Hariko's father has five nieces and nephews. They are Hariko's ....

   6 Jill's father married Wendy's mother. Jill's father is Wendy's ....

   7 Julie and Brett are divorced. Brett is Julie's ....

   8 Teresa's mother has two brothers. They are Teresa's ....

C Complete the questions. Use the simple present tense.

   1 A: Where .... ?
      B: My brother? He lives in Cuzco, Peru.

   2 A: What .... ?
      B: My sister? She's a nurse.

   3 A: How many .... ?
      B: I have two sons and a daughter.

   4 A: .... ?
      B: Cousins? Yes, I do. I have seven.

   5 A: Where .... ?
      B: My brother? He lives near me.

   6 A: .... ?
      B: Children? Yes. My sister has two daughters.

WRITING

Compare two people in your family. Write six statements about how they are similar and how they are different. Start like this:

My brother and his wife are similar in some ways,
but they are also very different . . .

WRITING BOOSTER p. 143
• Combining sentences with <u>and</u> or <u>but</u>
• Guidance for this writing exercise

For additional language practice . . .

♫ **TOP NOTCH** **POP** • Lyrics p. 149
"An Only Child"

DIGITAL SONG   DIGITAL KARAOKE

Enrique Iglesias's Family

Ronna Keitt
born 1964

Dr. Julio Iglesias Puga
1915–2005

(divorced)

María del Rosario
1919–2002

Jaime
born 2004

Ruth
born 2006

Miranda Rijnsburger
model
born 1965

Julio Iglesias
singer
born 1943

(divorced)

Isabel Preysler
TV host
born 1951

Carlos
born 1945

Miguel Alejandro
born 1997

Rodrigo
born 1999

Isabel
born 1971
(nickname: Chabeli)

Christian Altaba
businessman

Julio Jr.
singer/model
born 1973

Charisse Verhaert
model
born 1982

Enrique
singer
born 1975

Victoria and Cristina
born 2001

Guillermo
born 2007

Alejandro
born 2002

Sofia
born 2012

ORAL REVIEW

CONTEST Study the family tree. Who can answer this question first: How many sisters, brothers, half-sisters, and half-brothers do Enrique Iglesias and Julio Iglesias each have?

PAIR WORK Ask and answer questions about the family relationships. Use Who, What, When, and How many. For example:

Q: Who is Isabel Preysler?
A: She's . . .

GAME Choose one person's point of view. Describe "your extended family." Your partner guesses who you are. For example:

I am Julio Iglesias's daughter, and my uncle is Carlos.

✓ NOW I CAN

☐ Report news about relationships.
☐ Describe extended families.
☐ Compare people.
☐ Discuss family cultural traditions.

PREVIEW

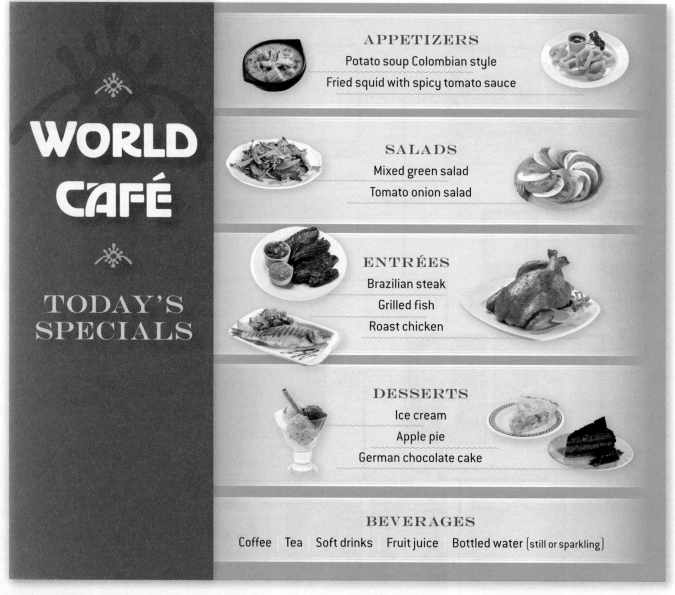

WORLD CAFÉ

TODAY'S SPECIALS

APPETIZERS
Potato soup Colombian style
Fried squid with spicy tomato sauce

SALADS
Mixed green salad
Tomato onion salad

ENTRÉES
Brazilian steak
Grilled fish
Roast chicken

DESSERTS
Ice cream
Apple pie
German chocolate cake

BEVERAGES
Coffee | Tea | Soft drinks | Fruit juice | Bottled water (still or sparkling)

A Read the menu. Circle the words that are new to you.

B ▶2:20 **VOCABULARY • Parts of a meal** Listen and repeat.

C **PAIR WORK** Which foods on the menu do you like? Are there any foods you don't like? Compare ideas with a partner.

D **NOTEPADDING** Write the name of at least one dish from your country for each category.

| an appetizer |
| an entrée (a main course) |
| a salad |
| a dessert |
| a beverage |

38 UNIT 4

E ▶ 2:21 **PHOTO STORY** Read and listen to someone ordering food in a restaurant.

Server:* Are you ready to order? Or do you need some more time?

Customer: I'm ready, thanks. I think I'll start with the potato soup. Then I'll have the roast chicken. What does that come with?

Server: It comes with a salad. And there's also a choice of vegetables. Tonight we have carrots or grilled tomatoes.

Customer: I'd like the carrots, please. Or, on second thought, maybe I'll have the tomatoes.

Server: Certainly. And anything to drink?

Customer: I'd like sparkling water, please. No ice.

*Server = waiter (man) or waitress (woman)

F **INFER MEANING** Check the correct answers, according to the Photo Story.

1 What does the customer order?
- ☐ an appetizer
- ☐ an entrée
- ☐ a dessert
- ☐ a beverage

2 What does the entrée come with?
- ☐ soup and salad
- ☐ salad and dessert
- ☐ carrots and grilled tomatoes
- ☐ salad and carrots or grilled tomatoes
- ☐ water

SPEAKING

A Practice ordering. First, use the menu from the World Café to complete the statements. Then read your statements to a partner. Your partner writes your order on his or her guest check.

1 I think I'll start with the ....

2 Then I'll have the ....

3 For my main course, I'd like the ....

4 For dessert, I'll have the ....

5 To drink, I'd like ....

B Now change roles. Listen to your partner's order and write it on your guest check.

Guest Check

Date	Table	Server	Check No. 2650

Tax

Total

GOAL Ask for a restaurant recommendation

DIGITAL FLASH CARDS

VOCABULARY *Categories of food*

A ▶2:22 Read and listen. Then listen again and repeat. Add another food to each category.

fruit
① apples ② bananas
③ grapes ④ oranges
mangoes ....

vegetables
⑤ carrots ⑥ peppers
⑦ broccoli ⑧ onions
....

meat
⑨ chicken ⑩ lamb
⑪ sausage ⑫ beef
....

seafood
⑬ fish ⑭ clams
⑮ shrimp ⑯ crab
⑰ squid ....

grains
⑱ pasta ⑲ rice
⑳ noodles ㉑ bread
....

dairy products
㉒ butter ㉓ cheese
㉔ milk ㉕ yogurt
....

oils
㉖ corn oil ㉗ olive oil
㉘ coconut oil
....

sweets
㉙ candy ㉚ pie
㉛ cake ㉜ cookies
....

B **EXPAND THE VOCABULARY** How many foods can you create? Use the Vocabulary. Follow the example.

1 orange **juice** *apple juice, mango juice* ....

2 tomato onion **salad** ....

3 apple **pie** ....

4 **grilled** fish ....

5 **fried** squid ....

6 potato **soup** ....

GRAMMAR *There is / There are with count and non-count nouns; Anything and nothing*

Use **there is** with non-count nouns and singular count nouns. Use **there are** with plural count nouns.

There's (some) milk and an apple in the fridge.
There are (some) cookies in the kitchen.

There isn't any cheese.
There aren't any bananas.

Questions

Is there any (*or* some) pasta?
Are there any (*or* some) noodles?
What kind of fruit **is there** in this fruit salad?
How many eggs **are there** in the fridge?

Use **Is there** with **anything** and **nothing**.

Is there **anything** to eat? (No, there is **nothing**.
OR No, there isn't **anything**.)

Remember:
• Count nouns name things you can count. They are singular or plural.
• Non-count nouns name things you cannot count. They are not singular or plural.
• Don't use <u>a</u>, <u>an</u>, or a number with non-count nouns: rice NOT a rice NOT rices

Be careful!

Use **nothing** in affirmative statements.
Use **anything** in negative statements.
There is **nothing**. NOT There isn't nothing.
There isn't **anything**. NOT There is anything.

GRAMMAR BOOSTER p. 128
• Expressing quantities
• <u>Some</u> and <u>any</u>
• <u>How much</u> / <u>how many</u>
• Count and non-count nouns
• Spelling rules

GRAMMAR PRACTICE Complete each statement or question with an affirmative or negative form of <u>there is</u> or <u>there are</u>.

DIGITAL
MORE
EXERCISES

1 .... some fish in the fridge.

2 .... onions in the salad.

3 .... some cheese for my sandwich?

4 .... any apple pies at the store?

5 .... some orange juice for your breakfast.

6 .... anything in the fridge?

7 .... anything to eat in this house!

8 .... any pasta for tonight's dinner.

CONVERSATION MODEL

A ▶2:23 Read and listen to someone asking for a restaurant recommendation.

A: Could you recommend a restaurant for this evening?

B: Sure. What are you in the mood for?

A: I don't know. Maybe a sandwich. I'm not very hungry.

B: Actually, there's a great place nearby. It's called Tom's. Would you like directions?

▶2:25 **Degrees of hunger**
- – not very hungry
- + really hungry
- +++ starving

B ▶2:24 **RHYTHM AND INTONATION** Listen again and repeat. Then practice the Conversation Model with a partner.

NOW YOU CAN Ask for a restaurant recommendation

DIGITAL
VIDEO

A **CONVERSATION ACTIVATOR** With a partner, change the Conversation Model. Ask for a recommendation for today, tonight, dinner, breakfast, or lunch. Recommend a restaurant from the map. Then change roles.

A: Could you recommend a restaurant for .... ?

B: .... What are you in the mood for?

A: I don't know. Maybe .... I'm ....

B: Actually, there's a great place nearby. It's called .... Would you like directions?

DON'T STOP!

Use the map and give directions to the restaurant you recommended.

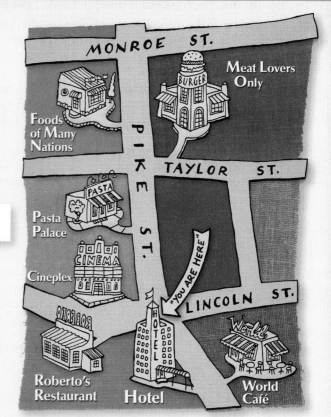

↻ RECYCLE THIS LANGUAGE.

Locations

around the corner	down the street from [the] __
across the street	between __ and __
across from [the] __	on the __ side of the street
near [the] __	

B **CHANGE PARTNERS** Practice the conversation again. Talk about other foods and restaurants.

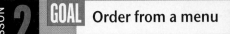

LESSON 2

GOAL Order from a menu

CONVERSATION MODEL

A ▶ 2:26 Read and listen to someone ordering dinner from a menu.

A: I'll have the pasta for my main course, please. What does that come with?

B: It comes with soup or a salad.

A: What kind of soup is there?

B: There's tomato soup or chicken soup.

A: I'd like the salad, please.

B: Certainly. And to drink?

A: Water, please.

B ▶ 2:27 **RHYTHM AND INTONATION** Listen again and repeat. Then practice the Conversation Model with a partner.

GRAMMAR *Definite article the*

Use the definite article the to name something a second time.

A: It comes with a salad.
B: OK. I'll have **the salad**.

Also use the to talk about something specific.

A: Would you like an appetizer? (not specific; general)
B: Yes. **The fried clams** sound delicious. (specific; they're on the menu)

A: I'm in the mood for seafood. (not specific; general)
B: Then I recommend **the grilled shrimp**. (specific; they're on the menu)

> **Remember:**
> Indefinite articles <u>a</u> and <u>an</u>:
> **a** salad   **an** appetizer
> **a** beverage   **an** entrée

> **GRAMMAR BOOSTER** p. 130
> • Non-count nouns: categories and verb agreement

A **UNDERSTAND THE GRAMMAR** Look at the Photo Story on page 39 again. Explain why the customer uses the definite article <u>the</u> in the following sentences.

1 "I think I'll start with <u>the</u> potato soup."

2 "Then I'll have <u>the</u> roast chicken."

3 "I'd like <u>the</u> carrots, please."

4 ". . . maybe I'll have <u>the</u> tomatoes."

B **GRAMMAR PRACTICE** Complete each conversation with <u>a</u>, <u>an</u>, or <u>the</u>.

1 **A:** What do you feel like eating tonight?

B: Well, ... seafood special sounds delicious.

2 **A:** I'm in the mood for .... really spicy dish.

B: Well, what about .... Thai chicken? Thai food is usually spicy.

3 A: There are two kinds of soup: chicken noodle and mixed vegetable.

   B: I think I'd like .... chicken noodle. I'm not a vegetable fan.

4 A: What would you like for your main course? We have .... nice grilled chicken special on .... menu tonight.

   B: That sounds good. I'll have .... chicken special.

PRONUNCIATION *The*

A ▶ 2:28 Compare the pronunciation of <u>the</u> before consonant and vowel sounds. Read and listen. Then listen again and repeat.

/ə/ (before consonant sounds)	/i/ (before vowel sounds)
the chicken	the orange juice
the soup	the onion soup
the juice	the apple juice
the hot appetizer	the appetizer
the fried eggs	the eggs

B Write a check mark if the <u>underlined</u> word begins with a vowel sound.

☑ the <u>egg</u> salad   ☐ the <u>apple</u> cake   ☐ the <u>clam</u> soup

☐ the <u>Chinese</u> fried squid   ☐ the <u>ice</u> cream   ☐ the <u>olive</u> oil

☐ the <u>tomato</u> sauce   ☐ the <u>chocolate</u> milk   ☐ the <u>grilled</u> fish

C **PAIR WORK** Now take turns saying each phrase. Be sure to use the correct pronunciation of <u>the</u>.

NOW YOU CAN Order from a menu

A **PAIR WORK** With a partner, invent a restaurant. Give your restaurant a name. Write foods on the menu. Include two or more choices for each category.

B **CONVERSATION ACTIVATOR** With a partner, change the Conversation Model, using your menu to order food. Pay attention to count and non-count nouns and definite and indefinite articles. Then change roles.

A: I'll have .... for my main course, please. What does that come with?

B: It comes with ....

A: What kind of .... is there?

B: ....

A: I'd like .... , please.

B: Certainly. And to drink?

A: .... , please.

DON'T STOP!
- Ask more questions.
- Order more food.
- Order a dessert.

C **EXTENSION** Bring in a real menu from your favorite restaurant. Use it to practice the conversation. Change partners and menus and practice the conversation again.

Welcome to

_____
(name of restaurant)

appetizers:
_____

soup:
_____

entrées:
_____

beverages:
_____

All entrées come with:
_____

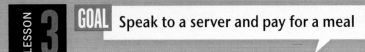
BEFORE YOU LISTEN

▶ 2:29 **VOCABULARY • *Communicating with a waiter or waitress***
Read and listen. Then listen again and repeat.

Excuse me!

We're ready to order.

I'm sorry. This isn't what I ordered.

We'll take the check, please.

Is the tip included?

Do you accept credit cards?

LISTENING COMPREHENSION

A ▶ 2:30 **LISTEN TO PREDICT**   Listen to the conversations in a restaurant. Then listen again
and predict the next thing you think the customer will say to the server. Explain your answers.

1 ☐ We'll take the check, please.
   ☐ Do you accept credit cards?
   ☐ We're ready to order.

2 ☐ This isn't what I ordered.
   ☐ We're ready to order.
   ☐ Is the tip included?

3 ☐ No, thanks. We'll take the check, please.
   ☐ Is the tip included?
   ☐ Do you accept credit cards?

4 ☐ Excuse me! This isn't what I ordered.
   ☐ Excuse me! We're ready to order.
   ☐ Excuse me! We'll take the check, please.

5 ☐ Excuse me!
   ☐ We'll start with the seafood soup, please.
   ☐ We'll take the check, please.

B **PAIR WORK**   Decide what to say to the server in each conversation. Then practice the conversation.

1 A: Oh, no! Take a look at this check!
   B: I'm not sure we have enough money.
      Excuse me! *Do you accept credit cards?*

2 A: Oh, no! They brought us onion soup. We
      ordered the tomato soup.
   B: You're right. Excuse me! ....

3 A: Oh, no! I left my money at home.
   B: Excuse me! ....

4 A: We can't order dessert. We don't have time.
   B: Right. Excuse me! ....

5 A: Here's the check. Do we need to leave a tip?
   B: I'll ask. Excuse me! ....

6 A: Where's the waitress? I'm starving.
   B: Excuse me! ....

NOW YOU CAN Speak to a server and pay for a meal

A **NOTEPADDING** Plan your meal. Read the menu and choose what you'd like to order. Write your choice for each category.

appetizer
soup
salad
main course
beverage
dessert

THE BISTRO

APPETIZERS

Crab cake   Mini lamb pies   Mixed grilled vegetables

SOUP

Spicy shrimp   Chicken noodle   Tomato

SALADS

Tomato pepper   Green bean   Pasta

ENTRÉES

All entrées include bread, soup or salad, vegetable, and coffee or tea.

Roast beef   Fried fish   Pasta with clam sauce

CHOICE OF VEGETABLES:

Broccoli   Grilled tomatoes   Potatoes (any style)

BEVERAGES

Bottled water (still or sparkling)   Soft drinks   Fruit juices   Tea   Coffee

DESSERTS

Ice cream sandwiches   Carrot cake   Mixed fruit salad   Fruit and cheese plate

B **GROUP WORK** Form groups of diners at tables, with some students as servers. Discuss the menu. Ask the server questions about the food. Order and pay for the meal.

RECYCLE THIS LANGUAGE.

Discuss food	Serve food	Order food	Pay for food
What are you in the mood for?	Are you ready to order?	Excuse me!	I'll / We'll take the check, please.
I'm in the mood for __.	Do you need more time?	I'm / We're ready.	Is the tip included?
There's __ on the menu.	That comes with __.	I'd like to start with __.	Do you accept credit cards?
The __ sound(s) delicious.	Would you like __?	I think I'll have __.	
What about __?	Anything to drink?	And then I'll have __.	
This isn't what I ordered.	And to drink?	Does that come with __?	
	And for your [entrée]?	What does that come with?	
		What kind of __ is there?	

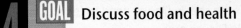

BEFORE YOU READ

A ▶2:31 **VOCABULARY** • *Adjectives to describe the healthfulness of food*
Read and listen. Then listen again and repeat.

DIGITAL FLASH CARDS

healthy   is good for you

unhealthy   is bad for you

fatty / high-fat   contains a lot of oil

low-fat   doesn't contain a lot of oil

salty   contains a lot of salt

sweet   contains a lot of sugar

high-calorie   can make you fat or overweight

low-calorie   is not going to make you fat

B **WARM-UP**   Do you like to eat at fast-food restaurants? Is it possible to get healthy food there? Use the Vocabulary as you express your opinion.

READING ▶2:32

DID YOU KNOW?

Just one super-sized fast-food meal can have more calories than you should eat in an entire day!

These tips can help you eat healthy meals and maintain a healthy weight when eating out and when eating at home.

Maintain a healthy weight.

When you eat out . . .

Control your portions. Many people eat larger portions than they need, especially when eating away from home. Order something small. Or ask for a half-portion. If you do order a large meal, take half of it home or split it with someone else at the table. Sharing food is also less expensive.

Avoid unhealthy snacks such as pizza, candy, and fast food. When you do get fast food, skip the fries and other high-calorie, fatty, or salty options.

Skip the fries.

Choose healthy options. Grilled chicken and fish are low-fat and low-calorie. If you really want some fried food, remove the breading from the food so it won't have so many calories.

And at home . . .

Avoid eating in front of the TV. If you eat while you are doing other things, it's easy to lose track of how much you are eating.

Eat slowly. Let your brain get the message that your stomach is full. Your brain needs about twenty minutes before it gets that message. If you eat fast, you will eat more food.

Eat more "veggies."

QUICK TIPS

- Try to avoid high-calorie cookies and cake for dessert. If you love sweets, try low-fat frozen yogurt or fruit for dessert instead. Yogurt and fruit are both sweet and healthy.

- Avoid adding sugar to your food and drinks.

For more information about healthy eating, visit *http://win.niddk.nih.gov*

A **UNDERSTAND FROM CONTEXT** Find the following words and phrases in the Reading and match them with their meanings. Then use the words to write your own sentences.

.... **1** "veggies"   **a** the amount you eat at one time

.... **2** "skip" or "avoid"   **b** not choose

.... **3** "portion"   **c** vegetables

.... **4** "split" or "share"   **d** choice

.... **5** "option"   **e** order one dish for two people

B **INFER INFORMATION** Which suggestions help you avoid eating too much fat? Which ones help you avoid too much sugar?

DIGITAL
MORE
EXERCISES

NOW YOU CAN Discuss food and health

A **FRAME YOUR IDEAS** Write a ✓ next to the foods you think are healthy. Write an ✗ next to the foods you think are not. Then discuss your answers with a partner. Explain why some of the foods are unhealthy.

> 66 French fries are not healthy. They're too fatty. 99

> 66 I agree. 99

☐ salad

☐ hot peppers

☐ pasta with sauce

☐ rice

☐ chicken

☐ pizza

☐ hamburgers

☐ french fries

nuts   chips
☐ snacks

☐ ice cream

B **NOTEPADDING** List other foods and drinks you think are good for you and bad for you.

Healthy foods	Unhealthy foods
oranges	salty foods, like potato chips

C **DISCUSSION** Now discuss food and health with your class. Suggest healthy eating tips. Use your lists.

Text-mining (optional)
Find and underline three words or phrases in the Reading that were new to you. Use them in your Discussion. For example: "a half-portion."

🔄 RECYCLE THIS LANGUAGE.

Categories of foods		Adjectives	Verbs
grains	meat	healthy / unhealthy	skip / avoid
seafood	sweets	good / bad for you	split / share
dairy products	fruit	high-calorie / low-calorie	
vegetables	oils	fatty / salty / sweet / spicy	

REVIEW

A ▶2:33 Listen to the conversations. Where are the people? Circle <u>at home</u> or <u>in a restaurant</u>. Then predict what each person will say next. Listen again and complete the statements.

1 The man and woman are (at home / in a restaurant).
I think he's going to ask, "Does dessert .... with my .... ?"

2 Caroline and her mom are (at home / in a restaurant).
Her mom is probably going to say, "But Caroline, ... are really ...."

3 The man and woman are (at home / in a restaurant).
It's possible that he's going to say, " .... the grilled ...."

4 The couple is (at home / in a restaurant).
It's possible that she's going to say, "Terrific! Let's .... an omelette and a salad. I'm really .... !"

B Write examples of foods for each category.

Spicy foods	Salty foods	Sweet foods	Fatty foods

C Write questions you can ask a waiter or a waitress. Begin each question with a capital letter and end with a question mark.

1 ....

2 ....

3 ....

4 ....

D Complete each sentence with an affirmative or negative form of <u>there is</u> or <u>there are</u>.

1 .... too much pepper in the soup. It's too spicy.

2 Excuse me. I'm looking for a restaurant. .... any good restaurants in the neighborhood?

3 .... any low-fat desserts on the menu?

4 .... an inexpensive restaurant nearby?

5 You should eat some fruit. .... some nice oranges on the kitchen table.

6 .... enough cheese in the fridge for two sandwiches. Let's go shopping.

7 I hope .... too much sugar in the cake. Sugar isn't good for you.

8 I'm in the mood for soup. What kind of soup .... on the menu?

WRITING

Write a short article for a travel blog about foods in your country.
Write at least five sentences, but write more if you can.

In my country we eat a lot of vegetables.

Vegetable soup is a very typical appetizer . . .

WRITING BOOSTER p. 143
• Connecting words or ideas: <u>and</u> and <u>in addition</u>
• Guidance for this writing exercise

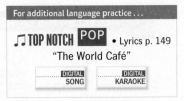

For additional language practice . . .

♫ **TOP NOTCH** **POP** • Lyrics p. 149
"The World Café"

DIGITAL SONG   DIGITAL KARAOKE

At a hotel

1

ORAL REVIEW

PAIR WORK Create conversations for the people in Pictures 1, 2, and 3. For example:

A: Can I help you?
B: Could you recommend a restaurant for ... ?

CONTEST Form teams. Each team takes turns making statements about the foods in Picture 4 with <u>there is</u> or <u>there are</u>. (Teams get one point for each correct statement.)

At a restaurant

2

3

4

NOW I CAN

☐ Ask for a restaurant recommendation.
☐ Order from a menu.
☐ Speak to a server and pay for a meal.
☐ Discuss food and health.

Technology and You

PREVIEW

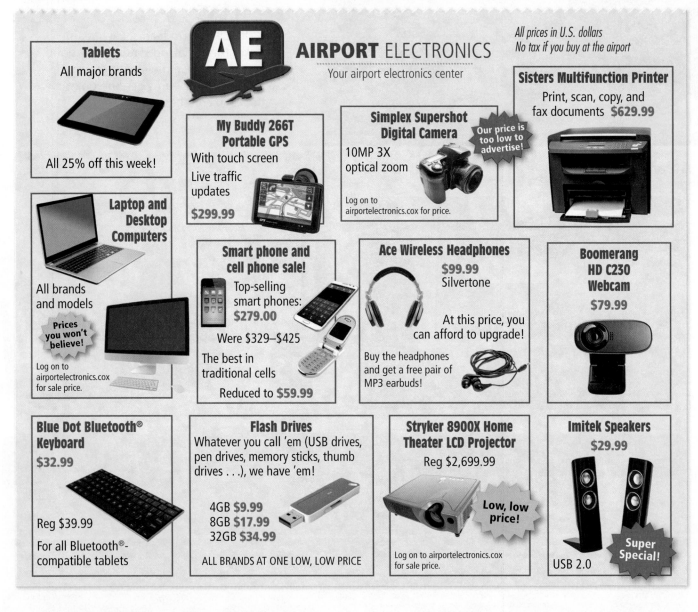

Tablets
All major brands
All 25% off this week!

AE AIRPORT ELECTRONICS
Your airport electronics center

All prices in U.S. dollars
No tax if you buy at the airport

Sisters Multifunction Printer
Print, scan, copy, and fax documents **$629.99**

My Buddy 266T Portable GPS
With touch screen
Live traffic updates
$299.99

Simplex Supershot Digital Camera
10MP 3X optical zoom
Log on to airportelectronics.cox for price.
Our price is too low to advertise!

Laptop and Desktop Computers
All brands and models
Prices you won't believe!
Log on to airportelectronics.cox for sale price.

Smart phone and cell phone sale!
Top-selling smart phones: **$279.00**
Were $329–$425
The best in traditional cells
Reduced to **$59.99**

Ace Wireless Headphones
$99.99
Silvertone
At this price, you can afford to upgrade!
Buy the headphones and get a free pair of MP3 earbuds!

Boomerang HD C230 Webcam
$79.99

Blue Dot Bluetooth® Keyboard
$32.99
Reg $39.99
For all Bluetooth®-compatible tablets

Flash Drives
Whatever you call 'em (USB drives, pen drives, memory sticks, thumb drives . . .), we have 'em!
4GB **$9.99**
8GB **$17.99**
32GB **$34.99**
ALL BRANDS AT ONE LOW, LOW PRICE

Stryker 8900X Home Theater LCD Projector
Reg $2,699.99
Low, low price!
Log on to airportelectronics.cox for sale price.

Imitek Speakers
$29.99
USB 2.0
Super Special!

A ▶3:02 **VOCABULARY • Electronic devices** Listen and repeat.

a tablet
a laptop (computer)
a desktop (computer)
a keyboard
a GPS
a smart phone
a cell phone
a flash drive
a digital camera
headphones
earbuds
a projector
a printer
a webcam
speakers

B PAIR WORK Look at the ad. Tell your partner about a product you need and why you need it.

" I need a webcam. I want to see my sister when we talk on the Internet. "

C ▶3:03 **PHOTO STORY** Read and listen to a conversation about a product that's not working.

Don: This printer's driving me crazy! It's on the blink again.

Erin: What's wrong with it?

Don: What *isn't* wrong with it? It's an absolute lemon.

Erin: No, seriously, what's the problem?

Don: Well, first off, the thing's an antique. It's ten years old.

Erin: OK. And . . . ?

Don: And it's *so* slow. It takes hours to print! And now it won't print at all!

Erin: Well, that *is* a problem. Maybe it's fixable. Let me have a look.

Don: Don't bother. It's not worth it. The thing's obsolete, anyway. It's not wireless, it has no scanner, it can't photocopy . . .

Erin: Sounds like you're ready for an upgrade. Airport Electronics is having a sale. Let's get you something more up-to-date!

D **FOCUS ON LANGUAGE** Find and underline the following statements in the Photo Story. Choose the statement that is closer in meaning to each one.

1 "This printer's driving me crazy!"
 a I love this printer!
 b I hate this printer!

2 "It's on the blink again."
 a The printer has a problem.
 b The printer is OK.

3 "It's an absolute lemon."
 a It's very bad.
 b It's very good.

4 " . . . the thing's an antique."
 a It's very new.
 b It's very old.

5 "Don't bother. It's not worth it."
 a I don't want to fix the printer.
 b I want to fix the printer.

6 " . . . you're ready for an upgrade."
 a You need a new printer.
 b Someone needs to fix your printer.

SPEAKING

A Read and listen to the words in Replacing products. Then choose three electronic products from the ad on page 50 you have but want to replace. Complete the chart with the name of the product and the reason you want to replace it.

▶3:04 **Replacing products**
broken doesn't work
obsolete hard to use because the technology is old
up-to-date uses new or recent technology
defective a new product with a problem

	Products	Why do you want to replace them?
1	My GPS.	It's broken.

	Products	Why do you want to replace them?
1		
2		
3		

B **DISCUSSION** Use your chart to discuss the products you need. Explain why you need to replace them.

GOAL Recommend a brand or model

CONVERSATION MODEL

A ▶3:05 Read and listen to someone suggest a brand and a model.

A: Hey, Rachel. What are you doing?

B: I'm uploading a video.

A: What kind of camcorder do you have?

B: It's a Vista, but I need a new one. Mine's obsolete! Any suggestions?

A: What about the Alton? I hear the MX2 is great. And it's inexpensive.

B: Really?

A: You know, I'm going shopping at the mall after work. Would you like to come along?

▶3:07 **Positive descriptions**
pretty good ☺
great ☺☺
terrific ☺☺☺
awesome ☺☺☺☺

a camcorder

B ▶3:06 **RHYTHM AND INTONATION** Listen again and repeat. Then practice the Conversation Model with a partner.

GRAMMAR *The present continuous: Review*

Use the present continuous for actions in progress now and for future plans.

Actions in progress
A: What **are** you **doing** right now?
B: I'**m downloading** a song.

Future plans
A: What **are** you **doing** tomorrow?
B: I'**m buying** a new camera.

Questions

Are you **looking** for a new printer? (Yes, I am. / No, I'm not.)
Are they **buying** a GPS? (Yes, they are. / No, they're not.)
Is he **using** his tablet? (Yes, he is. / No, he's not.)
Where **are** you **going**? (To Technoland.)
When **is** she **getting** a new laptop? (Next week.)
Who'**s buying** a new keyboard? (My wife.)

GRAMMAR BOOSTER p. 130
The present continuous:
• Spelling rules
• Form and usage rules

A FIND THE GRAMMAR Find and underline three sentences with the present continuous in the Conversation Model.

B UNDERSTAND THE GRAMMAR Write <u>now</u> next to the sentences that describe an action in progress and <u>future</u> next to those that describe a future plan.

future. **1** What <u>are</u> you <u>doing</u> this weekend?
.... **2** I'm busy this morning. I'<u>m answering</u> e-mails.
.... **3** He'<u>s leaving</u> in ten minutes. Hurry!
.... **4** Josh isn't home. He'<u>s shopping</u> for a laptop.
.... **5** They'<u>re eating</u> with us on Friday.
.... **6** The printer'<u>s not working</u> again.

PRONUNCIATION *Intonation of questions*

▶3:08 Listen and check for rising or falling intonation. Then take turns saying each question with a partner.

1 What are you doing?
2 Are you buying a computer?
3 What time are you going?
4 Is she looking for a new printer?

VOCABULARY *Collocations for using electronic devices*

A ▶ 3:09 Read and listen. Then listen again and repeat.

| take a picture / photo | upload a photo | make a video | scan a document | make a photocopy |

B **VOCABULARY / GRAMMAR PRACTICE** Complete the conversations, using the present continuous and the names of electronic devices from the list.

1 A: What .... (you / scan)?

B: The pictures for our presentation.

A: Great! Tell me when you finish. I need the .... , too.

2 A: Hi, Tom. .... (you / take) lots of pictures of Paris?

B: Oh, hi, Diane. Yes, I am. I'm using my new ....

A: E-mail me one of the Eiffel Tower, OK?

3 A: Hey, Melanie! What .... (you / do) here?

B: I'm shopping for a new ....

A: Me, too! Our old one is broken, and .... (I / make) a video of my daughter's birthday party next week.

4 A: Wow! My sister .... (upload) some great pictures onto FaceSpace. Look! Here come some new ones.

B: Pass me your .... so I can see.

5 A: Oh, no! I need 100 copies of the meeting agenda right away, and there's no time.

B: What's the problem?

A: Marie is at the .... She .... (make) copies of the sales results.

> camcorder
> camera
> laptop
> photocopier / copier
> scanner

NOW YOU CAN Recommend a brand or model

A **CONVERSATION ACTIVATOR** With a partner, change the Conversation Model. Use these ads or ones from a newspaper or online store. Change the activity and the adjective. Then change roles.

A: Hey, ... What are you doing?

B: I'm ....

A: What kind of .... is that?

B: It's a .... , but I really need a new one. This one's .... Any suggestions?

A: What about the .... ? I hear the .... is .... And it's ....

B: Really?

A: You know, I'm going shopping .... Would you like to come along?

DON'T STOP!

Accept or decline the invitation.
Great! I'd love to go.
I'd love to go, but ___.

B **CHANGE PARTNERS** Discuss other products and suggest other brands or models.

On sale
Printmore
Model 900S

Up-to-date!
Sounder
Model 88

New!
VistaPic
Model LX 10

Fast!
MyPhone
Model TT

Inexpensive!
HighTone
Model 2400

Easy to use
Vidiot
Model XOX

Activities
- listen to (an audiobook / music)
- scan (a document / a picture)
- print (instructions / a map)
- take pictures
- make a video
- upload (a photo /a video)

GOAL Express sympathy for a problem

CONVERSATION MODEL

A ▶3:10 Read and listen to people discussing a problem.

A: Hi, Ed. How's it going?

B: Fine, thanks. But my microwave's not working again.

A: Again? I'm sorry to hear that. What brand is it?

B: A Quickpoint. It's a piece of junk.

B ▶3:11 **RHYTHM AND INTONATION** Listen again and repeat.
Then practice the Conversation Model with a partner.

▶3:12 **Ways to sympathize**	▶3:13 **Negative descriptions**	
I'm sorry to hear that.	a piece of junk	awful
That's too bad.	pretty bad	horrible
That's a shame.	terrible	a lemon
Oh, no!		

VOCABULARY *Household appliances and machines*

DIGITAL FLASH CARDS

A ▶3:14 Read and listen. Then listen again and repeat.

1 a food processor

2 a hair dryer

3 a pressure cooker

4 a dishwasher

5 a coffee maker

6 a rice cooker

7 a fan

8 a stove   **9** an oven

10 a juicer

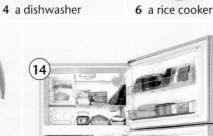

14 a freezer

16 an air conditioner

11 a washing machine
12 a dryer

13 a blender

14 a freezer
15 a refrigerator / a fridge

17 a vacuum cleaner

B Classify the Vocabulary by purpose. Write examples of appliances in each category.

For cleaning or washing	For food preparation	For cooking	For storage

C ▶ 3:15 **LISTEN TO PREDICT** Listen and write the name of the appliance. Then listen again and predict what the other person will say. Check the box.

1 appliance: ....
☐ Is it fixable?
☐ Sure. No problem.

2 appliance: ....
☐ It's an air conditioner.
☐ It's a Cool Wave.

3 appliance: ....
☐ It's not working?
☐ About thirty, I think.

4 appliance: ....
☐ Oops! Sorry about that.
☐ Sounds great!

5 appliance: ....
☐ Just use a little more water.
☐ I think the machine is defective.

6 appliance: ....
☐ Yeah. I'm so glad I bought it!
☐ I think it's time for an upgrade.

7 appliance: ....
☐ That's a shame. It's a lemon.
☐ Wow. That sounds great.

8 appliance: ....
☐ I'm sorry to hear that.
☐ Sure. Just a second.

NOW YOU CAN Express sympathy for a problem

A **NOTEPADDING** Think of five products and brands that don't work well. Write them on the notepad.

	Product	Brand
1	a hair dryer	Beautiful Hair

	Product	Brand
1		
2		
3		
4		
5		

B **CONVERSATION ACTIVATOR** With a partner, change the Conversation Model, using one of the products from your notepad. Express sympathy. Use the negative descriptions from page 54. Then change roles.

A: Hi, ... How's it going?
B: .... But my .... 's not working again.
A: Again? .... What brand is it?
B: .... It's ....

DON'T STOP!
Say more about the product.

RECYCLE THIS LANGUAGE.
It's driving me crazy!
It's on the blink.
It's an absolute lemon.
The thing's an antique.
It's broken / obsolete / defective.

C **CHANGE PARTNERS** Practice the conversation again. Use another product from your notepad.

BEFORE YOU LISTEN

A ▶3:16 **VOCABULARY • *Ways to state a problem***
Read and listen. Then listen again and repeat.

DIGITAL
FLASH
CARDS

The window **won't open / close**.

The iron **won't turn on**.

The air conditioner **won't turn off**.

The fridge is **making a funny sound**.

The toilet **won't flush**.

The sink **is clogged**.

B Write the names of machines, appliances, and devices that sometimes . . .

1 won't open or close. ....

2 won't turn on or off. ....

3 make a funny sound. ....

LISTENING COMPREHENSION

A ▶3:17 **LISTEN FOR DETAILS** Listen to the conversations. Write the room number for each complaint. Then listen again and write another problem for each room, using the Vocabulary.

GUEST COMPLAINT LOG

ROOM	PROBLEM	OTHER PROBLEMS?
203	The toilet won't stop flushing.	
	The fridge isn't working.	
	The sink is clogged.	

B **DISCUSSION** Which problems on the guest complaint log are serious? Which are not serious? Explain your reasons.

> ❝ It's serious when the sink is clogged. Water on the floor is very bad. ❞

Complain when things don't work

A **NOTEPADDING** Find all the problems in the hotel. Write the problems on the notepad.

Room / Place	Problem(s)

B **ROLE PLAY** Create conversations between the front desk clerk and the hotel guests about things that don't work.

> Hello. Front desk. Can I help you?

> I'm in the elevator. It's not working and the doors won't open.

> I'll send someone right away.

🔄 **RECYCLE THIS LANGUAGE.**

Telephone language	State a problem	Respond
Hello?	__ won't open / close.	What's the problem?
This is room __.	__ won't turn on / off.	I'm sorry to hear that.
Bye.	__ won't flush / stop flushing.	Oh, no!
	__ isn't working.	Well, that <u>is</u> a problem.
	__ is clogged.	
	__ is making a funny sound.	
	__ is driving me crazy.	
	__ is broken.	

GOAL Describe features of products

BEFORE YOU READ

WARM-UP What kinds of features are important to you in a new product?

READING ▶ 3:18

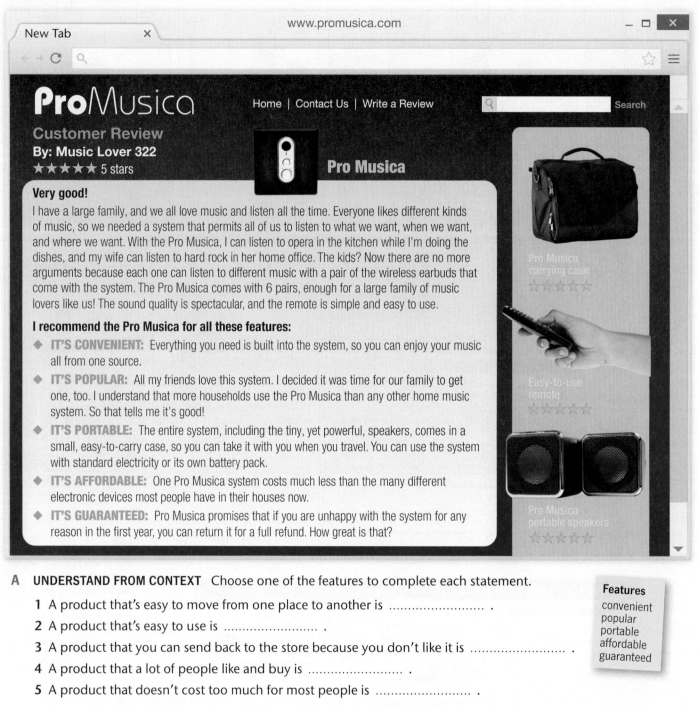

www.promusica.com

New Tab ×

ProMusica

Home | Contact Us | Write a Review   Search

Customer Review
By: Music Lover 322
★★★★★ 5 stars   **Pro Musica**

Very good!
I have a large family, and we all love music and listen all the time. Everyone likes different kinds of music, so we needed a system that permits all of us to listen to what we want, when we want, and where we want. With the Pro Musica, I can listen to opera in the kitchen while I'm doing the dishes, and my wife can listen to hard rock in her home office. The kids? Now there are no more arguments because each one can listen to different music with a pair of the wireless earbuds that come with the system. The Pro Musica comes with 6 pairs, enough for a large family of music lovers like us! The sound quality is spectacular, and the remote is simple and easy to use.

I recommend the Pro Musica for all these features:
◆ **IT'S CONVENIENT:** Everything you need is built into the system, so you can enjoy your music all from one source.
◆ **IT'S POPULAR:** All my friends love this system. I decided it was time for our family to get one, too. I understand that more households use the Pro Musica than any other home music system. So that tells me it's good!
◆ **IT'S PORTABLE:** The entire system, including the tiny, yet powerful, speakers, comes in a small, easy-to-carry case, so you can take it with you when you travel. You can use the system with standard electricity or its own battery pack.
◆ **IT'S AFFORDABLE:** One Pro Musica system costs much less than the many different electronic devices most people have in their houses now.
◆ **IT'S GUARANTEED:** Pro Musica promises that if you are unhappy with the system for any reason in the first year, you can return it for a full refund. How great is that?

Pro Musica carrying case ☆☆☆☆☆

Easy-to-use remote ☆☆☆☆☆

Pro Musica portable speakers ☆☆☆☆☆

A UNDERSTAND FROM CONTEXT Choose one of the features to complete each statement.

1 A product that's easy to move from one place to another is ....
2 A product that's easy to use is ....
3 A product that you can send back to the store because you don't like it is ....
4 A product that a lot of people like and buy is ....
5 A product that doesn't cost too much for most people is ....

Features
convenient
popular
portable
affordable
guaranteed

B ACTIVATE LANGUAGE FROM A TEXT What is good about the Pro Musica? Use the features Vocabulary and your own ideas to explain your answer.

DIGITAL
MORE
EXERCISES

C ▶3:19 **LISTEN TO CLASSIFY** Listen to the radio advertisements for some crazy gadgets. Check all the adjectives that describe each product.

gadget /ˈɡædʒɪt/ n.
a small tool or machine that makes a particular job easier

Longman Dictionary of American English

1 "The Sleeper"

☐ convenient ☐ popular
☐ portable ☐ affordable

2 "Cool as a Cucumber"

☐ convenient ☐ popular
☐ portable ☐ affordable

3 "The Scribbler"

☐ guaranteed ☐ convenient
☐ affordable ☐ popular

D ▶3:20 **PAIR WORK** Choose one of the three gadgets. Listen again and take notes. Then try to convince your partner to buy the product. Use the features Vocabulary from the Reading on page 58.

NOW YOU CAN Describe features of products

A **NOTEPADDING** Choose one good product that you own and one bad product (appliances, electronic products, gadgets, etc.). Write the good or bad features on the notepad.

Product	Brand	Good or bad features
smart phone	Link	affordable / up-to-date
scanner	Blue Bird	obsolete / makes a funny sound

Product	Brand	Good or bad features

B **DISCUSSION** Describe the good and bad features of your products. Tell your classmates about all the good and bad features. Use your notepad.

❝ I like the new Link smart phone. It's affordable and up-to-date. ❞

❝ I don't recommend the Blue Bird scanner. It's obsolete. ❞

Text-mining (optional)
Find and underline three words or phrases in the Reading that were new to you. Use them in your Discussion. For example: "simple and easy to use."

RECYCLE THIS LANGUAGE.

Negative descriptions		Positive descriptions		Ways to sympathize
awful	terrible	great	guaranteed	I'm sorry to hear that.
broken	an antique	terrific	affordable	That's too bad.
defective	a lemon	awesome	convenient	That's a shame.
horrible	a piece of junk	fast	pretty good	Oh, no!
not fixable	drives me crazy	popular	up-to-date	Maybe it's fixable.
obsolete	won't start			You're ready for an upgrade.
on the blink	makes a funny sound			
slow	won't turn off			

A ▶3:21 Listen to the conversations about problems with products and appliances. Write a sentence to describe each problem.

Example: _The fan won't turn on._

1 ....

2 ....

3 ....

4 ....

B Complete each conversation with a question in the present continuous. (More than one question is possible.)

1 A: Where .... tomorrow?
  B: We're going to My Electronics World. Want to come along?

2 A: .... you .... a new camera?
  B: Yes. Our old camera is obsolete. It's not digital.

3 A: When .... ?
  B: He's getting a smart phone for his birthday.

4 A: What .... ?
  B: Tomorrow? We're fixing our old printer.

5 A: What .... ?
  B: Right now? We're eating dinner.

C Complete each statement. Circle the correct word or phrase.

1 This new toilet is (defective / portable). It doesn't flush.

2 I think my TV is (affordable / broken). I hope it's fixable.

3 Your computer is probably (obsolete / up-to-date). You should get a new one.

4 This scanner is really a piece of junk. I think we should get (an upgrade / a lemon).

D Add products, appliances, and gadgets to the chart. Write at least three in each category. (Some products may go in more than one category.)

Machines that are:						
Portable	Popular	Convenient	Affordable	Good for communication	Good for entertainment	Good for cooking
					tablet	

WRITING

Write a review of a product, appliance, or gadget that you use. It can be a good product or a bad one. You can give it 1–5 stars.

Star ratings
★ not so great
★★ OK
★★★ good
★★★★ very good
★★★★★ awesome

☆ ☆ ☆ ☆

I have a Hot Spot dishwasher and . . .

WRITING BOOSTER p. 144
• Placement of adjectives: before nouns and after the verb <u>be</u>
• Guidance for this writing exercise

For additional language practice . . .

♫ TOP NOTCH **POP** • Lyrics p. 149
"It's Not Working Again"
DIGITAL SONG   DIGITAL KARAOKE

Picture 1

ORAL REVIEW

CONTESTS

1 Form teams. Study the products in Pictures 1 and 2 for two minutes. Then close your books. With your team, make a list of what you saw. The team with the most correct words after one minute wins.

2 Form teams. Study the names and activities in Picture 1 for two minutes. Then close your books. Ask another team <u>yes</u> / <u>no</u> questions about the people, using the present continuous. (Teams get one point for each correct answer.) For example:

Q: Is Jane studying?
A: No, she isn't.

PAIR WORK

1 Point to the people in Picture 1. Ask and answer information questions, using the present continuous. For example:

Q: What's Jane doing?
A: She's listening to music.

2 Create a conversation for the people in Picture 2. For example:

A: The Disheroo is affordable. And it's guaranteed.
B: But they say it's a piece of junk. Let's get the Kitchenmax. It's expensive, but it's very popular.

Picture 2

Kleen Up
$60.00
Convenient and portable!

Blackmore
$449.99

Cool Rite
$429.99

Lane
$1,199.00
New!

Kitchenmax
$900.00
Popular!

Disheroo
$499.99
Guaranteed for 5 years!

✓ NOW I CAN

☐ Recommend a brand or model.
☐ Express sympathy for a problem.
☐ Complain when things don't work.
☐ Describe features of products.

UNIT 6 Staying in Shape

COMMUNICATION GOALS
1 Plan an activity with someone.
2 Talk about habitual activities and plans.
3 Discuss fitness and eating habits.
4 Describe your routines.

PREVIEW

How many calories can you burn in one hour?

Activity	Calories
play basketball	572
go running	572
go swimming	572
play soccer	501
go bike riding	500
do aerobics	429
play golf	322
go dancing	322
go walking	250
take a shower	248
lift weights	214
cook dinner	179
clean the house	179
go shopping	164
study English	128
talk on the phone	71
watch TV	71
sleep	64

CALORIES*   0   100   200   300   400   500   600

*Based on a person weighing 150 pounds / 68.2 kilograms

Running on a treadmill is a good way to burn calories.

A ▶ 3:24 **VOCABULARY • Activities** Look at the graph. Then listen and repeat.

B **CLASS SURVEY** According to the graph, approximately how many calories do <u>you</u> burn every day? Find out who in your class burns more than 1,500 calories a day.

C ▶ 3:25 **PHOTO STORY** Read and listen to people talk about playing tennis.

Lynn: Hi, Joy! What are you up to?

Joy: Lynn! How are you? I'm playing tennis, actually. In the park.

Lynn: You play tennis? I didn't know that.

Joy: I do. About three times a week. Do you play?

Lynn: Not as much as I'd like to.

Joy: Well, why don't we meet at the park on Saturday?

Lynn: This coming Saturday? Sorry, I can't. I have to work. What about Sunday?

Joy: Perfect. Hey, how about your husband? Can he come, too?

Lynn: Ken? No way. He's a total couch potato. He just watches TV and eats junk food. He's so out of shape.

Joy: Too bad. My husband's crazy about tennis.

Lynn: Listen. I'm on my way home right now. Let's talk tomorrow. OK?

Joy: Terrific.

D **FOCUS ON LANGUAGE** Look at the underlined expressions in the Photo Story. Use the context to help you choose the correct meaning of the following sentences.

1 What are you up to?
  a What are you doing?
  b Where are you going?

2 Why don't we play tennis sometime?
  a Can you explain why we don't play tennis?
  b Would you like to play tennis sometime?

3 My husband is really out of shape.
  a My husband doesn't exercise.
  b My husband exercises a lot.

4 I'm crazy about tennis.
  a I hate tennis.
  b I love tennis.

5 I'm on my way to the park.
  a I'm going to the park right now.
  b I'm going to go to the park this afternoon.

SPEAKING

A **PERSONALIZE** Look at the activities on page 62. List the activities you do . . .

every day	every weekend	once a week	almost never	never

B **PAIR WORK** Compare activities with a partner.   ❝ What do you do every weekend? ❞   ❝ Me? I go shopping. ❞

GOAL Plan an activity with someone

GRAMMAR *Can* and *have to*

can

Use *can* + the base form of a verb for possibility.

We **can stay** out late tonight. There are no classes tomorrow morning.
I'm too busy this afternoon. I **can't play** golf.
Mona **can meet** us at the park, but her husband **can't**.

Questions

Can you **go** running tomorrow at 3:00? (Yes, I can. / No, I can't.)

> **Remember:** *Can* + base
> form also expresses ability.
>
> We **can speak** English.
> They **can't play** piano.

have to

Use *have to* or *has to* + the base form of a verb for obligation.

I | have to / don't have to | work late tonight.

She | has to / doesn't have to | meet her cousin at the airport at 3:00.

Questions

Do they **have to work** tomorrow? (Yes, they do. / No, they don't.)
Does he **have to go** to class now? (Yes, he does. / No, he doesn't.)

> **Usage:** When declining an invitation,
> use *have to* to provide a reason.
>
> Sorry, I **can't**. **I have to work** late.

> **GRAMMAR BOOSTER** p. 132
>
> Can and have to:
> • Form and common errors
> • Information questions
> Can and be able to: present and past forms

A FIND THE GRAMMAR Look at the Photo Story on page 63 again. Find one statement using *can't* to decline an invitation. Find one example of *have to* to provide a reason. Find one question using *can* for possibility.

B GRAMMAR PRACTICE Read the sentences carefully. Then complete each sentence with *can* or a form of *have to*.

1 I'd like to go out tonight, but we have a test tomorrow. I ....
   (study)

2 Audrey .... us for lunch today. She .... her boss write a report.
   (not / meet)   (help)

3 Good news! I .... late tonight. We .... together at 6:00.
   (not / work)   (go running)

4 My sister .... at the mall today. She .... to the doctor.
   (not / go shopping)   (go)

5 Henry .... to Toronto next week, so he .... golf with us.
   (go)   (not / play)

6 Sorry, I .... to aerobics class tonight. I .... with my boss.
   (not / go)   (meet)

C GRAMMAR PRACTICE Write three questions using *can* and three questions using a form of *have to*. Then practice asking and answering the questions with a partner.

PRONUNCIATION *Can / can't*

A ▶3:26 Read and listen to the pronunciation and stress of *can* and *can't*. Then listen again and repeat.

/kən/ I can **call** you today.   /kænt/ I can't **call** you tomorrow.

B ▶3:27 Listen to the statements and check *can* or *can't*. Then listen again and repeat each statement.

1 ☐ can ☐ can't   3 ☐ can ☐ can't   5 ☐ can ☐ can't
2 ☐ can ☐ can't   4 ☐ can ☐ can't   6 ☐ can ☐ can't

CONVERSATION MODEL

A ▶3:28 Read and listen to two people plan an activity together.

A: Hey, Gary. Why don't we go running sometime?

B: Great idea. When's good for you?

A: Friday morning at 9:00?

B: Sorry, I can't. I have to work on Friday.

A: Well, how about Sunday afternoon at 2:00?

B: That's good for me. See you then.

B ▶3:29 **RHYTHM AND INTONATION** Listen again and repeat. Then practice the Conversation Model with a partner.

NOW YOU CAN Plan an activity with someone

A **NOTEPADDING** Write your schedule for this weekend in the daily planner. (Use page 62 for ideas.)

	Friday	Saturday	Sunday
9:00	go running	visit Mom	

Daily Planner

	Friday	Saturday	Sunday
9:00			
11:00			
1:00			
3:00			
5:00			
7:00			

B **CONVERSATION ACTIVATOR** Now personalize the Conversation Model with a partner, using your daily planners. Suggest an activity, a day, and a time. Then change roles.

A: Hey, ... Why don't we .... sometime?

B: .... When's good for you?

A: .... ?

B: Sorry, I can't. I have to ....

A: Well, how about .... ?

B: ....

DON'T STOP!
- Suggest other times and activities.
- Discuss where to meet.

C **CHANGE PARTNERS** Practice the conversation again. Plan other activities. Use your daily planner to respond.

GOAL **Talk about habitual activities and plans**

VOCABULARY *Places for sports and exercise*

A ▶3:30 Read and listen. Then listen again and repeat.

a pool

an athletic field

a golf course

a track

a tennis court

a park

a gym

B **PAIR WORK** Tell your partner what you do at these places.

❝ I play soccer at the athletic field next to the school. ❞

GRAMMAR *The present continuous and the simple present tense: Review*

The present continuous (for actions in progress and future plans)	**The simple present tense** (for frequency, habits, and routines)	▶3:31 **Frequency adverbs**
I'm making dinner right now. They're swimming at the pool in the park. He's meeting his friends for lunch tomorrow.	I make dinner at least twice a week. They usually swim at the pool on Tuesdays. He hardly ever meets his friends for dinner.	100% always almost always usually / often / generally sometimes / occasionally hardly ever 0% never
Questions Are you going running tomorrow? What time are you playing tennis today?	**Questions** Do you always play golf on Saturdays? How often do you lift weights?	

Be careful!
Don't use the present continuous with frequency adverbs.
  Don't say: ~~She's never playing~~ tennis.
Don't use the present continuous with <u>have</u>, <u>want</u>, <u>need</u>, or <u>like</u>.
  Don't say: ~~She's liking~~ the gym.

GRAMMAR BOOSTER p. 133
The simple present tense:
• Non-action verbs
• Placement of frequency adverbs
• Time expressions

A **VOCABULARY / GRAMMAR PRACTICE** Tell a partner how frequently you play sports or exercise at the places from the Vocabulary.

❝ I almost always go to my gym on Fridays. ❞

❝ There's a pool near my house, but I hardly ever go swimming there. ❞

B GRAMMAR PRACTICE Complete the sentences. Use the simple present tense or the present continuous.

1 Brian can't answer the phone right now.

....
      he / study

2 How often .... walking?
                     she / go

3 .... tennis this weekend.
       we / play

4 .... weights three times a week.
       he / lift

5 .... lunch. Can they call
      they / make
you back?

6 How often .... the house?
               you / clean

7 .... aerobics every day.
      I / do

8 .... shopping tonight.
      she / go

C ▶3:32 **LISTEN TO ACTIVATE GRAMMAR** Listen to the conversations. Circle the frequency adverb that best completes each statement.

1 She (often / hardly ever / never) plays golf.

2 He (often / sometimes / always) goes to the gym four times a week.

3 She (often / sometimes / never) plays tennis in the park.

4 He (always / often / never) goes swimming.

5 She (always / sometimes / never) rides her bike on weekends.

CONVERSATION MODEL

A ▶3:33 Read and listen to two people talk about habitual activities and future plans.

A: Hey, Nancy. Where are you off to?

B: Hi, Trish. I'm going to the gym.

A: Really? Don't you usually go there on weekends?

B: Yes. But not this weekend.

A: How come?

B: Because *this* weekend I'm going to the beach.

B ▶3:34 **RHYTHM AND INTONATION** Listen again and repeat. Then practice the Conversation Model with a partner.

C FIND THE GRAMMAR Look at the Conversation Model again. Underline one example of the simple present tense and two examples of the present continuous. Which one has future meaning?

NOW YOU CAN Talk about habitual activities and plans

A CONVERSATION ACTIVATOR With a partner, change the Conversation Model, using a different place from the Vocabulary. Then change roles.

A: Hey, ... Where are you off to?
B: Hi, ... I'm going to the ....
A: Really? Don't you usually go there .... ?
B: Yes. But not this ....
A: How come?
B: Because *this* .... I'm ....

DON'T STOP!

Say more about your activities.
I'm going to the gym. I have an aerobics class.
I'm going to the park. I'm playing tennis with my friend Julie.

Invite your partner to do something.
Why don't we ____ sometime?

B CHANGE PARTNERS Practice the conversation again. Use a different place and plan.

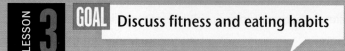

GOAL Discuss fitness and eating habits

BEFORE YOU LISTEN

WARM-UP In your opinion, is it important for people to stay in shape? Why? What do people have to do to stay in shape?

LISTENING COMPREHENSION

A ▶3:35 **LISTEN FOR MAIN IDEAS** Listen to people talk about their fitness and eating habits. Check the box next to the name if the person exercises regularly.

Mark Newell ☐   Rika Oinuma ☐   Richard Clark ☐

B ▶3:36 **LISTEN FOR DETAILS** Now listen again and check each person's habits.

	Mark	Rika	Richard
1 goes to a gym	☐	☐	☐
2 takes exercise classes	☐	☐	☐
3 exercises outside	☐	☐	☐
4 avoids grains	☐	☐	☐
5 avoids desserts	☐	☐	☐
6 avoids fatty foods	☐	☐	☐
7 eats smaller portions	☐	☐	☐
8 eats a lot of seafood	☐	☐	☐
9 eats slowly	☐	☐	☐

C **DISCUSSION**

1 In your opinion, which of the three people have good fitness and eating habits? Explain.

2 Whose habits are like your own? Explain.

DIGITAL VIDEO COACH

PRONUNCIATION *Third-person singular -s: Review*

A ▶3:37 Read and listen to the three third-person singular endings. Then listen again and repeat.

B **PAIR WORK** Take turns making statements about the three people's habits. Use the information in the chart in Listening Comprehension Exercise B. Pay attention to third-person singular endings.

/s/	/z/	/ɪz/
sleeps	goes	watches
eats	plays	exercises
works	avoids	munches

" Rika exercises outside every day. "

A FRAME YOUR IDEAS Take the health survey.

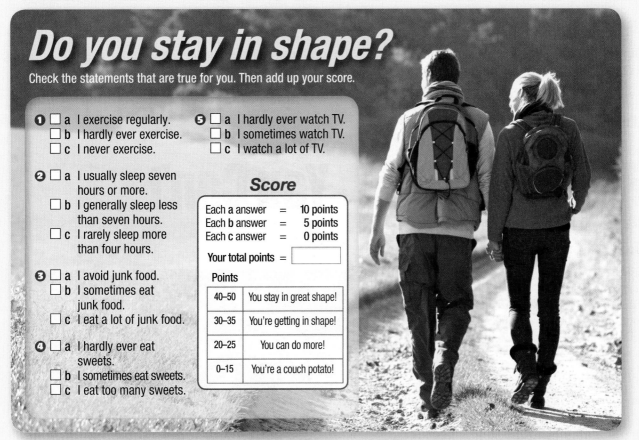

Do you stay in shape?

Check the statements that are true for you. Then add up your score.

① ☐ **a** I exercise regularly.
☐ **b** I hardly ever exercise.
☐ **c** I never exercise.

② ☐ **a** I usually sleep seven hours or more.
☐ **b** I generally sleep less than seven hours.
☐ **c** I rarely sleep more than four hours.

③ ☐ **a** I avoid junk food.
☐ **b** I sometimes eat junk food.
☐ **c** I eat a lot of junk food.

④ ☐ **a** I hardly ever eat sweets.
☐ **b** I sometimes eat sweets.
☐ **c** I eat too many sweets.

⑤ ☐ **a** I hardly ever watch TV.
☐ **b** I sometimes watch TV.
☐ **c** I watch a lot of TV.

Score

Each **a** answer = 10 points
Each **b** answer = 5 points
Each **c** answer = 0 points

Your total points = ☐

Points

40–50	You stay in great shape!
30–35	You're getting in shape!
20–25	You can do more!
0–15	You're a couch potato!

B PAIR WORK Compare your survey answers and scores.

C GROUP WORK Walk around the classroom and ask questions. Write names and take notes on the chart.

DON'T STOP!

Ask for more information:
Why are you out of shape?
What junk foods do you eat?
Where do you exercise?

Find someone who . . .	Name	Other information
stays in great shape.	Toni	goes running every day

Find someone who . . .	Name	Other information
stays in great shape.		
is out of shape.		
eats a lot of junk food.		
avoids sweets.		
avoids fatty foods.		
never sleeps more than four hours.		

D DISCUSSION Now discuss fitness and eating habits. Tell your classmates about the people on your chart.

 Toni stays in great shape. She goes running every day. ""

BEFORE YOU READ

PREVIEW Look only at the title, photos, and captions. What do these two people have in common? What do you think they have to do in order to participate successfully in their sports?

READING ▶ 3:38

When You Think You Can't...

Mark Zupan

▇ When he was eighteen years old, a terrible accident made Mark Zupan a quadriplegic and changed his life forever. At first, he could hardly move his arms or legs normally. However, after a lot of hard work, he was able to use his arms to move his wheelchair, and he could even stand for a short time and take a few slow steps. Zupan—or Zup to his friends—became a quad rugby champion, helping his team win a gold medal in the Paralympic Games. "I dream about running all the time," he says, "but you can't live in the past."

Today, Zupan frequently gives talks and raises money for his sport and appears in movies and TV shows. Anyone who spends time with him forgets that he's in a wheelchair. He lifts weights at the gym every day, drives a car, and goes to rock concerts. "A lot of people think quadriplegics can't do anything," he says. To stay in shape, Zupan is careful about his diet and avoids unhealthy and fatty foods. "Just think of me as a human being and an athlete. Because that's who I am."

Zupan became a quad rugby champion.

Bethany Hamilton

▇ At the age of thirteen, surfer Bethany Hamilton had a dream. She wanted to be a champion in her sport. But she lost her left arm when she was attacked by a shark. A month later, she was surfing again.

Today, she's a professional competitive surfer. Because she can only use one arm, she has to use her legs more to help her go in the right direction. Hamilton practices every day at the beach. She has a prosthetic arm, but she rarely uses it, and never when she's surfing.

Hamilton often appears on TV. She wants to help other people follow their dreams, even when they face great difficulties. "People can do whatever they want if they just set their hearts to it, and just never give up."

In 2011, Hollywood made a movie about her experience. Bethany has a happy life and got married in 2013.

Hamilton was attacked by a tiger shark when she was thirteen.

A **INFER INFORMATION** Complete the paragraph about Mark Zupan. Use <u>can</u>, <u>can't</u>, or <u>has to</u>.

Zupan .... spend most of his time in a wheelchair, but he .... stand up
               1   2
and take a few steps for a short time. He .... go walking or running, but he
                                          3
.... play quad rugby. He .... be careful about his diet so he doesn't get out of
    4   5
shape. He doesn't have complete use of his hands, but he .... lift weights.
                                                          6
He .... drive a car using his feet, but he .... use his hands. A lot of people
    7   8
think quadriplegics .... do anything, but Zupan proves that they ....
                     9   10

B **SUMMARIZE** First, complete the paragraph about Bethany Hamilton. Use the simple present tense or the
present continuous. Then write a similar paragraph, summarizing Mark Zupan's routines.

When she surfs, Hamilton .... her legs to help her go in the right direction.
                          1 use
She .... a prosthetic arm, but she hardly ever .... it.
    2 have   3 wear
She .... regularly with the world's top professional women surfers.
    4 compete
In the photo on page 70, she .... against other surfers with two arms.
                             5 compete
She .... a T-shirt and .... on her surfboard. Hamilton
    6 wear   7 stand
.... to help other people with difficult experiences follow their dreams.
    8 want

DIGITAL
MORE
EXERCISES

NOW YOU CAN Describe your routines

A **NOTEPADDING** Write some notes about your daily routines.

	List some things you usually do . . .	List some things you . . .
	• in the morning.	• can't do every day. Explain why.
	• in the afternoon.	• have to do every day. Explain why.
	• in the evening.	• don't have to do every day. Explain why.

B **PAIR WORK** Interview your partner about his or
her daily routines. Then describe your partner's
daily routines to your classmates.

> My partner usually gets up at 7:00. But on
> Saturdays, she doesn't have to get up early.

REVIEW

A ▶3:39 Listen to the conversations. Check the statements that are true.

1 ☐ He doesn't exercise regularly.
  ☐ He avoids junk food.
  ☐ He never watches TV.

2 ☐ She's in great shape.
  ☐ She hardly ever goes swimming.
  ☐ She exercises regularly.

3 ☐ He exercises regularly.
  ☐ He has to be careful about calories.
  ☐ He can eat everything he wants.

4 ☐ Dave Heeley can't use his legs.
  ☐ Dave Heeley can't see.
  ☐ Dave Heeley doesn't need help.

B What activities can you do at these places? Write sentences with <u>can</u>.

an athletic field	*I can play . . .*
a gym	
a park	

C Change each statement to a <u>yes</u> / <u>no</u> question. Begin each question with a capital letter and end with a question mark.

1 You have to go home early. *Do you have to go home early?*

2 Magda has to see a doctor this afternoon. ....

3 Jonah can meet us at the mall at 6:00. ....

4 I have to exercise every day. ....

5 My friends can come to the park after school. ....

6 Your husband has to work late tonight. ....

7 Lance's sisters have to avoid sweets. ....

D Answer the questions with real information. Use the simple present tense or the present continuous in your answer.

1 How often do you go to English class?
  YOU ....

2 What do you usually do on weekends?
  YOU ....

3 What are you doing this weekend?
  YOU ....

WRITING

Describe your exercise and health habits.

I'm not in very good shape, but I exercise three times a week now. I'm also very careful about the foods I eat . . .

WRITING BOOSTER p. 145
• Punctuation of statements and questions
• Guidance for this writing exercise

For additional language practice . . .

♫ TOP NOTCH **POP** • Lyrics p. 150
"A Typical Day"

DIGITAL SONG   DIGITAL KARAOKE

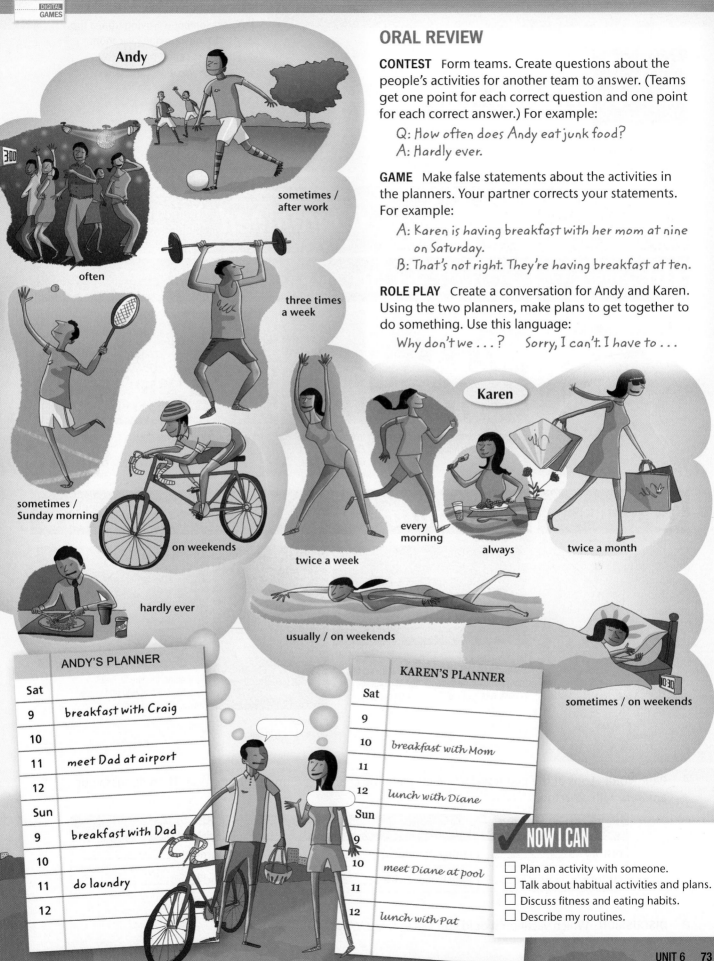

ORAL REVIEW

CONTEST Form teams. Create questions about the people's activities for another team to answer. (Teams get one point for each correct question and one point for each correct answer.) For example:

Q: How often does Andy eat junk food?
A: Hardly ever.

GAME Make false statements about the activities in the planners. Your partner corrects your statements. For example:

A: Karen is having breakfast with her mom at nine on Saturday.
B: That's not right. They're having breakfast at ten.

ROLE PLAY Create a conversation for Andy and Karen. Using the two planners, make plans to get together to do something. Use this language:

Why don't we . . . ?   Sorry, I can't. I have to . . .

Andy

sometimes / after work

often

three times a week

sometimes / Sunday morning

on weekends

twice a week

Karen

every morning

always

twice a month

hardly ever

usually / on weekends

sometimes / on weekends

ANDY'S PLANNER

Sat	
9	breakfast with Craig
10	
11	meet Dad at airport
12	
Sun	
9	breakfast with Dad
10	
11	do laundry
12	

KAREN'S PLANNER

Sat	
9	
10	breakfast with Mom
11	
12	lunch with Diane
Sun	
9	
10	meet Diane at pool
11	
12	lunch with Pat

✓ NOW I CAN

- ☐ Plan an activity with someone.
- ☐ Talk about habitual activities and plans.
- ☐ Discuss fitness and eating habits.
- ☐ Describe my routines.

COMMUNICATION GOALS

1 Greet someone arriving from a trip.
2 Ask about someone's vacation.
3 Discuss vacation preferences.
4 Describe vacation experiences.

UNIT 7 On Vacation

PREVIEW

Travel Specials | *Guaranteed* Your money refunded if your flight or cruise is canceled.

10 Days

TOUR EUROPE
• Fly to London on July 15.
• Fly back home from London on July 25.

See a play in London's West End or visit the British Museum.

In Paris, visit the Eiffel Tower and enjoy France's excellent food.

Go shopping in Milan. Explore the ruins of the Colosseum in Rome.

Go to a concert in Vienna and enjoy the city's famous desserts.

11 Nights

Hawaiian Cruise
• Leave from Vancouver, Canada on July 15.
• Fly back home from Honolulu on July 26.

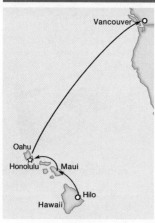

On board the ship . . .
Swim in a beautiful heated pool. Eat in one of many fantastic restaurants. And at night, see a popular movie or a show . . . or go dancing!

In Hawaii . . .
Go snorkeling in Oahu.

Walk along the scenic black sand beaches of Hilo and enjoy Hawaii's natural beauty.

A **PAIR WORK** Look at the two travel ads. Complete the chart by writing <u>tour</u> or <u>cruise</u>. Then discuss your answers with a partner.

In your opinion, which travel special would be good for someone who likes . . .		
history? _____	family activities? _____	entertainment? _____
culture? _____	physical activities? _____	good food? _____

B **DISCUSSION** Which vacation would you like to take? Why?

C ▶ 4:02 **PHOTO STORY** Read and listen to a phone call from someone returning from a trip.

Kate: Hi, Nancy. We're home!

Nancy: Kate! When did you get back?

Kate: Late last night.

Nancy: So, did you have a good time?

Kate: It was fantastic! Phil and I really needed a vacation!

Nancy: So, tell me all about your cruise!

Kate: Well, the ship was huge. And they had everything: incredible food, entertainment, family activities . . . There were always lots of things to do.

Nancy: And what was Hawaii like?

Kate: Hawaii? Just awesome! The beaches were really beautiful.

Nancy: Cool!

Kate: And in Maui we went windsurfing, and in Oahu, we went snorkeling. But most of the time we just sat on the beach and enjoyed the view.

Nancy: Now that's *my* kind of vacation!

Kate: I can't wait for the next one.

Nancy: Well, welcome home.

D **FOCUS ON LANGUAGE** Look at the underlined words and expressions in the Photo Story. Find:

1 an expression that means "come home." ....

2 four adjectives that mean "great." ....

E **THINK AND EXPLAIN** Complete the statements.

1 When Nancy says, "Now that's *my* kind of vacation!" she means ....

2 When Kate says, "I can't wait for the next one," she means ....

F **PERSONALIZATION** Which part of Kate's vacation is *your* kind of vacation? Explain your reasons.

SPEAKING

PAIR WORK Complete the questionnaire. Then tell your partner what you usually do on your vacations. Ask about your partner's vacations.

Where do you usually go for vacation?

☐ I stay home.
☐ I visit my family.
☐ I go to the beach.
☐ I go to another city.
☐ I go to another country.
☐ Other _____

GOAL Greet someone arriving from a trip

GRAMMAR *The past tense of be: Review*

Statements	Questions
I He She It **was** **wasn't** on vacation.	**Was** your flight late? (Yes, it was. / No, it wasn't.) **Were** there lots of people on the train? (Yes, there were. / No, there weren't.)
We You They **were** **weren't** on vacation.	Where **was** your brother yesterday? (At the Smith Museum.) When **were** you in Seoul? (Last month.) Who **was** with you on the train? (My girlfriend.) Who **were** your parents with? (My grandfather.)
	How **was** the food at the airport? (It wasn't very good.) How **were** the activities on your cruise? (They were great.) How long **was** the tour? (It was three hours.) How long **were** you on the bus? (For two hours.)

Contractions
wasn't = was not
weren't = were not

GRAMMAR BOOSTER p. 135
• The past tense of be: form

A FIND THE GRAMMAR Look at the Photo Story on page 75. Find five examples of the past tense of be.

B GRAMMAR PRACTICE Complete the conversations, using was, were, wasn't, or weren't.

1 A: Welcome back! How .... the drive?
B: Not great. There .... too many buses.
A: Too bad. .... you alone?
B: No, I .... My brother .... with me.

2 A: How long .... your flight?
B: Six hours. But it .... OK. The flight
attendants .... very nice.
A: Good. .... there a lot of passengers?
B: No, there ....

3 A: Where .... you last Thursday?
B: I .... in London.
A: No kidding! Who .... with you?
B: My cousin. He .... in London, too.
A: So how long .... you there?
B: We .... in London for four days.

4 A: When .... Kayla on vacation?
B: Actually, she and her husband .... in
Hawaii two weeks ago.
A: Wow! .... they on a cruise?
B: Yes. They .... It .... a six-day cruise.

VOCABULARY *Adjectives to describe trips; intensifiers*

A ▶4:03 Read and listen. Then listen again and repeat.

▶4:04 **Intensifiers**
so
very
really
pretty
quite
kind of

Our bus trip was so **scary**.

The flight was very **bumpy**.

It was really **short**. / It was really **long**.

Our train trip was pretty **scenic**.

It was quite **comfortable**.

The drive was kind of **boring**.

B **PAIR WORK** Use the adjectives from the Vocabulary to describe a trip you took. Use different intensifiers.

> " Last year, I went to a small town in the mountains. The bus trip was **really bumpy**. "

CONVERSATION MODEL

A ▶4:05 Read and listen to someone greet a person arriving from a trip.

A: Welcome back!

B: Thanks.

A: So, how was the flight?

B: It was pretty comfortable, actually.

A: That's good! Hey, can I give you a hand?

B: It's OK. I'm fine.

A: Are you sure?

B: Absolutely. Thanks!

▶4:07

Decline help	Accept help
It's OK. I'm fine.	Thank you!
No, thanks. I'm OK.	That's really nice!

B ▶4:06 **RHYTHM AND INTONATION** Listen again and repeat. Then practice the Conversation Model with a partner.

NOW YOU CAN Greet someone arriving from a trip

A **CONVERSATION ACTIVATOR** With a partner, change the Conversation Model, using a different adjective and intensifier and the past tense of <u>be</u>. Accept or decline help. Then change roles.

A: Welcome back!

B: ....

A: So, how was the .... ?

B: It was .... , actually.

A: That's .... ! Hey, can I give you a hand?

B: ....

Responses

comfortable scenic short	That's good!
boring bumpy scary long	That's too bad!

DON'T STOP!

Ask your partner other questions about the trip.
Were there a lot of people on the __?
How long was the __?

B **CHANGE PARTNERS** Practice the conversation again. Greet someone arriving from another type of trip. Ask more questions.

GOAL Ask about someone's vacation

CONVERSATION MODEL

A ▶4:08 Read and listen to someone describe a vacation.

A: Were you on vacation?

B: Yes, I was. I went to Paris.

A: No kidding! Did you have a good time?

B: Fantastic. I stayed in a really nice hotel and ate at some wonderful restaurants.

A: That sounds nice. Tell me more.

B ▶4:09 **RHYTHM AND INTONATION** Listen again and repeat. Then practice the Conversation Model with a partner.

GRAMMAR *The simple past tense: Review*

I He / She / It We / You / They	**arrived** at three. **didn't arrive** until six.

Did he **have** a good time? (Yes, he did. / No, he didn't.)
Did they **get** back late? (Yes, they did. / No, they didn't.)

Where **did** she **go**? (She went to Italy.)
When **did** his flight **leave**? (At 6:45.)
What **did** you **do** every day? (We visited museums.)
How many countries **did** they **see**? (Three.)
Who **did** you **go** with? (I went with my sister.)

BUT Who **went** with you? (My sister went with me.)

Regular verbs: spelling

+ ed	**+ d**	**+ ied**
visit**ed**	arriv**ed**	study ➜ stud**ied**
watch**ed**	chang**ed**	try ➜ tr**ied**
play**ed**	lik**ed**	

▶4:10 **Some irregular verbs**

buy	**bought**	get	**got**	sleep	**slept**
do	**did**	go	**went**	spend	**spent**
drink	**drank**	have	**had**	swim	**swam**
eat	**ate**	leave	**left**	take	**took**
find	**found**	see	**saw**		
fly	**flew**	sit	**sat**		

See page 122 for a more complete list.

GRAMMAR BOOSTER p. 135
• The simple past tense: more on spelling, usage, and form

A **FIND THE GRAMMAR** Look at the Photo Story on page 75 again. Circle all verbs in the simple past tense. Which are irregular verbs?

B **GRAMMAR PRACTICE** Complete Ida's post with past forms of the verbs.

Ida Graham

Greetings! We .... here yesterday evening, and I .... the whole flight.
   1   fly   2   sleep
I .... that! We .... a taxi from the airport to our hotel and ....
   3   need   4   take   5   find
a nice restaurant for a late dinner. Early this morning, we .... in the pool. For
                                                                    6   swim
breakfast, we .... some local dishes and .... some fantastic fruit juice.
               7   have   8   drink
Then, before noon, we .... along the beach. We .... people selling
                        9   walk   10   see
coconuts right from the trees, but we .... any. When we ....
                                         11   not / try   12   get
back to the hotel, we .... lunch. In the afternoon, we .... shopping
                        13   eat   14   go
and .... some cool things. We .... a lot on this trip, and we
      15   buy   16   do
.... a great time! So what .... while I .... on vacation?
   17   have   18   you / do   19   be

C **PAIR WORK** Write five questions about Ida's vacation, using the simple past tense. Then practice asking and answering your questions with a partner.

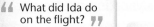

" What did Ida do on the flight? "

" She slept. "

D **GRAMMAR PRACTICE** Imagine that you just got back from one of the vacations on page 74. Write at least five sentences describing what you did, using the simple past tense.

DIGITAL
MORE
EXERCISES

We left Vancouver on July 15. . . .

DIGITAL
VIDEO
COACH

PRONUNCIATION *The simple past tense ending: Regular verbs*

A ▶ 4:11 Look at the chart and listen to the pronunciation of the simple past tense ending -<u>ed</u>. Then listen again and repeat. Practice saying each word on your own.

/d/	/t/	/ɪd/
played	cooked	wait·ed
rained	watched	need·ed
studied	introduced	visit·ed

Be careful!
played = /pleɪd/   NOT   ~~pleɪ·yɪd~~/
cooked = /kʊkt/   NOT   ~~/kʊk·ɪd~~/
BUT waited = /weɪ·tɪd/

B ▶ 4:12 Listen to the verbs. Circle the -<u>ed</u> ending you hear.

1 tried /d/ /t/ /ɪd/   **3** needed /d/ /t/ /ɪd/   **5** danced /d/ /t/ /ɪd/

2 walked /d/ /t/ /ɪd/   **4** checked /d/ /t/ /ɪd/   **6** wanted /d/ /t/ /ɪd/

NOW YOU CAN Ask about someone's vacation

DIGITAL
VIDEO

A **CONVERSATION ACTIVATOR** With a partner, change the Conversation Model, using the vacation ads or your own ideas. Then change roles.

A: Were you on vacation?
B: Yes, I was. I ....
A: No kidding! Did you have a good time?
B: .... I .... and ....
A: That sounds .... Tell me more.

DON'T STOP!
- Tell your partner more about your vacation.
- Ask and answer more questions, using the simple past tense.
  Did you ___?   Where ___?
  What ___?   When ___?

🔄 **RECYCLE THIS LANGUAGE.**

incredible	terrific	awesome
fantastic	wonderful	cool
great	perfect	nice

B **CHANGE PARTNERS** Practice the conversation again, using a different vacation.

THAILAND
GO SNORKELING.
EAT THAI FOOD.

VALLE NEVADO, CHILE
GO SKIING DURING THE DAY.
GO DANCING AT NIGHT.

NEW YORK
SEE THE EMPIRE STATE BUILDING.
GO SHOPPING.

ATHENS, GREECE
VISIT THE PARTHENON.
GO ON A CRUISE.

BEFORE YOU READ

DIGITAL FLASH CARDS

A ▶4:13 **VOCABULARY** • *Adjectives for vacations* Read and listen. Then listen again and repeat.

Also remember:
awesome
beautiful
boring
cool
excellent
famous
fantastic
great
incredible
nice
perfect
scenic
terrific
wonderful

It was **relaxing**.

It was **exciting**.

It was **interesting**.

It was **unusual**.

B **PAIR WORK** Use the Vocabulary to describe one of your vacations. Use intensifiers from page 76 in your description.

66 Last year, I went to the beach. It was **so relaxing** and . . . 99

READING ▶4:14

Now that's MY kind of vacation!

Our clients share their favorite destinations among our popular vacation packages.

Vacation 1

For your health and well-being

The perfect getaway—the Bagus Jati spa and hotel in Bali, Indonesia

"At home, we work really hard, and we needed some time off. Our spa vacation to Bali was perfect! They really took care of us. My wife and I enjoyed excellent healthy meals and some interesting workshops on healthy living and meditation. It was so quiet there! For exercise, we went swimming and bike riding. I'm going back again next year!"

—Jason K. (Seattle, U.S.)

Vacation 2

5... 4... 3... 2... 1...
BUNGEE!!!

Do you dare? A total adventure at Victoria Falls

"What a brilliant vacation! Located on the Zambezi River on the border between Zambia and Zimbabwe, the Victoria Falls are fantastic. You can't believe how big they are——absolutely huge! The idea of bungee jumping there was really scary. But then I tried it, and it was so exciting. I want to do it again! If you like adventure, this is the place to go."

—Paula B. (Dartford, U.K.)

Vacation 3

GLOBAL VILLAGE PROJECT

Learn about another culture and help the world.

"My vacation to Tajikistan lasted twenty-six days, and we helped build new homes for ten of those days. On the other days, we went sightseeing and bought souvenirs. The people were incredibly nice, and I loved the food. There were twelve other volunteers on this trip. The work was actually fun, and we got to know each other pretty well. In the end we felt really good. I'd definitely do it again!"

—Arturo Manuel R. (Monterrey, Mexico)

A **SUPPORT AN OPINION** Write check marks for the adjectives that, in your opinion, describe each vacation from the Reading. (Or add your own adjectives.) Explain your reasons.

> ❝ I think Vacation 1 is really boring because . . . ❞

	exciting	relaxing	unusual	interesting	scenic	boring	other adjectives
Vacation 1							
Vacation 2							
Vacation 3							

B **DRAW CONCLUSIONS** Choose one or more vacations from page 80 for each person. Explain why.

❝ I love to meet new people and learn how to do new things. ❞

❝ I love all kinds of sports and physical activities. ❞

❝ I like to go to places where other people don't go. ❞

❝ I need a vacation where I don't have to do *anything*. ❞

DIGITAL
MORE
EXERCISES

NOW YOU CAN Discuss vacation preferences

A **FRAME YOUR IDEAS** Complete the questionnaire. Then compare answers with a partner.

Need a Vacation? Check all your preferences:

How often do you go on vacation? ☐ never ☐ once or twice a year ☐ more than twice a year

I prefer vacations that are . . .

☐ relaxing
☐ exciting
☐ interesting
☐ unusual
☐ inexpensive
☐ scenic
☐ other _____

I like vacations with . . .

☐ lots of history and culture
☐ natural beauty
☐ sports and physical activities
☐ family activities
☐ great entertainment
☐ people who speak my language

☐ top-notch hotels
☐ great food
☐ warm weather
☐ scenic beaches
☐ friendly people
☐ other _____
_____
_____

Do you need a vacation right now? ☐ Not really. ☐ Maybe. ☐ You bet I do!

B **DISCUSSION** Now discuss your vacation preferences. Tell your classmates what's important to you.

> **Text-mining (optional)**
> Find and underline three words or phrases in the Reading that were new to you. Use them in your Discussion. For example: "time off."

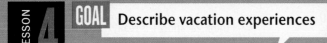
BEFORE YOU LISTEN

A ▶4:15 **VOCABULARY** • *Bad and good travel experiences* Read and listen. Then listen again and repeat.

Bad experiences

The weather was **horrible**. **really awful**. **pretty bad**. **terrible**.

The people were so **unfriendly**. **cold**.

They lost my luggage.

Someone stole my wallet.

Good experiences

The weather was **amazing**. **fantastic**. **terrific**. **wonderful**.

The people were so **friendly**. **warm**.

They found my luggage.

Someone returned my wallet.

B Look at the pictures. Complete the sentences.

1 ....*Someone stole*.... my purse. 2 The food .... 3 The waiters ....

4 The entertainment .... 5 .... my luggage.

LISTENING COMPREHENSION

A ▶ 4:16 **LISTEN FOR MAIN IDEAS** Listen to the conversations. Check whether, at the end of the vacation, the person had a good experience or a bad one.

1 ☐ a good experience ☐ a bad experience   3 ☐ a good experience ☐ a bad experience

2 ☐ a good experience ☐ a bad experience   4 ☐ a good experience ☐ a bad experience

B ▶ 4:17 **LISTEN FOR DETAILS** Listen again and complete the statements about each vacation.

1 The food was (very good / really awful).
 The room was (OK / pretty bad).
 The entertainment was (really bad / amazing).

2 The hotel was (terrible / terrific).
 Someone stole their (car / luggage).
 Miami was (horrible / wonderful).

3 He didn't have any more (clothes / money).
 The people were very (nice / cold).
 The hotel was (great / terrible).
 Someone stole his (passport / laptop).

4 The food was (fantastic / pretty bad).
 The people were (cold / nice).
 The vacation was too (short / long).

NOW YOU CAN   Describe vacation experiences

A **NOTEPADDING** Make a list of some of your good and bad vacation experiences.

Good experiences	Bad experiences
I went to Bangkok, and the people were really friendly.	When I went to Los Angeles, they lost my luggage.

Good experiences	Bad experiences

Ideas for topics
- your luggage / wallet / laptop / phone
- the trip / flight / train / bus
- the weather
- the food
- the hotel / front desk clerk / server
- the activities / shopping
- the entertainment
- the airport / museum / beach

B **PAIR WORK** Now tell your partner about the good and bad vacation experiences on your notepad. Ask questions about your partner's experiences.

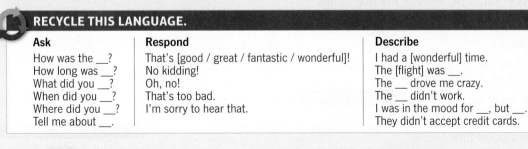

RECYCLE THIS LANGUAGE.

Ask	Respond	Describe
How was the __?	That's [good / great / fantastic / wonderful]!	I had a [wonderful] time.
How long was __?	No kidding!	The [flight] was __.
What did you __?	Oh, no!	The __ drove me crazy.
When did you __?	That's too bad.	The __ didn't work.
Where did you __?	I'm sorry to hear that.	I was in the mood for __, but __.
Tell me about __.		They didn't accept credit cards.

A ▶4:18 Listen to each person describe a good or bad vacation experience. Write the number of the speaker next to the type of trip he or she took.

☐ a drive   ☐ a train trip   ☐ a flight   ☐ a beach vacation

B ▶4:19 Listen again. Circle the adjective that best describes each experience.

1 Her trip was very (short / scary / scenic).   **3** Her trip was pretty (short / scary / boring).

2 His trip was quite (scary / unusual / relaxing).   **4** His trip was really (short / scenic / boring).

C Complete each information question, using the simple past tense.

1 A: .... on vacation?
    B: We went to Greece.

2 A: .... stay there?
    B: Two weeks.

3 A: .... every day?
    B: We walked along the beach and enjoyed the sun.

4 A: .... get back home?
    B: Last night.

D Complete each statement or question about vacations. Use past tense forms.

1 (we / buy) .... a lot of fantastic things on our vacation.

2 (where / you / eat) .... dinner every night?

3 (we / sleep) .... right on the beach. (it / be) .... so relaxing.

4 (my sister / get back) .... last weekend. (she / have) ....
a terrific time.

5 (my friend / eat) .... some fantastic food on her trip to Hong Kong.

6 (when / she / arrive) .... at the hotel?

7 (I / have) .... a terrible time. (the people / be) .... quite unfriendly.

8 (we / see) .... an interesting play in London. And (it / be) ....
pretty inexpensive.

9 (my wife and I / go running) .... every morning on the beach
during our vacation.

10 (my brother / meet) .... some unusual people on his trip.

WRITING

Write about a vacation you took. Answer the questions.

- When did you go?
- Where did you go?
- How long did you stay?
- How was the trip?
- How was the weather?
- What did you do?
- Did you have a good time?

WRITING BOOSTER p. 146
- Time order
- Guidance for this writing exercise

In 2014, I went on a great trip to . . .

For additional language practice . . .

🎵 **TOP NOTCH** **POP** • Lyrics p. 150
"My Dream Vacation"

| DIGITAL SONG | DIGITAL KARAOKE |

ORAL REVIEW

CONTEST Form two teams. Each team looks at the vacation pictures below and takes turns making a statement about the vacation, using the past tense. Continue until one team cannot say anything more. (Each team has thirty seconds to make a statement.)

ROLE PLAY Create a conversation for the two women on February 5. Start like this:

Were you on vacation?

PAIR WORK Choose one of the vacation pictures. Create a conversation for the people. Start with one of these, or your own idea:

- *Can I give you a hand?*
- *This bed is awful!*
- *Excuse me!*
- *This is so relaxing.*

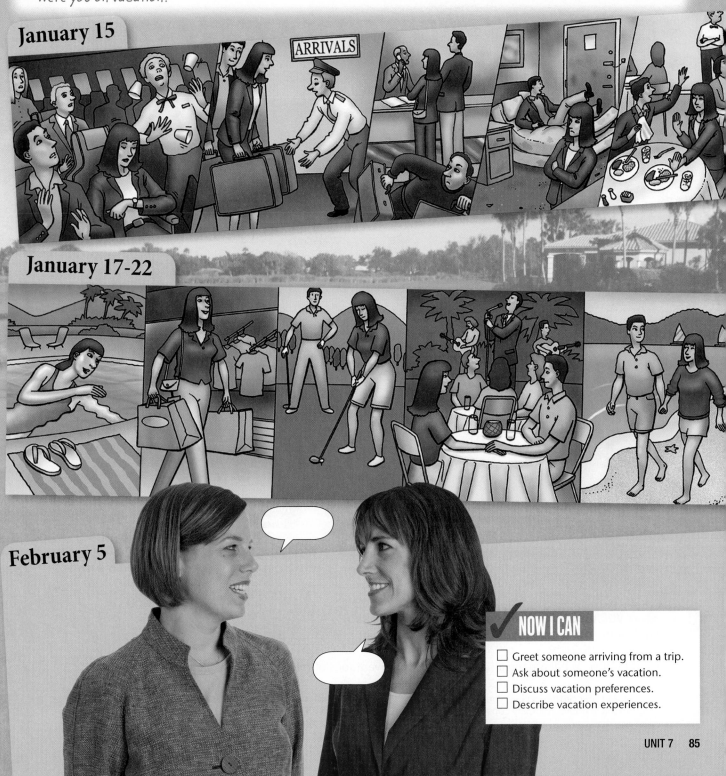

January 15

January 17-22

February 5

✓ NOW I CAN

- ☐ Greet someone arriving from a trip.
- ☐ Ask about someone's vacation.
- ☐ Discuss vacation preferences.
- ☐ Describe vacation experiences.

UNIT 8 Shopping for Clothes

COMMUNICATION GOALS

1 Shop and pay for clothes.
2 Ask for a different size or color.
3 Navigate a mall or department store.
4 Discuss clothing do's and don'ts.

PREVIEW

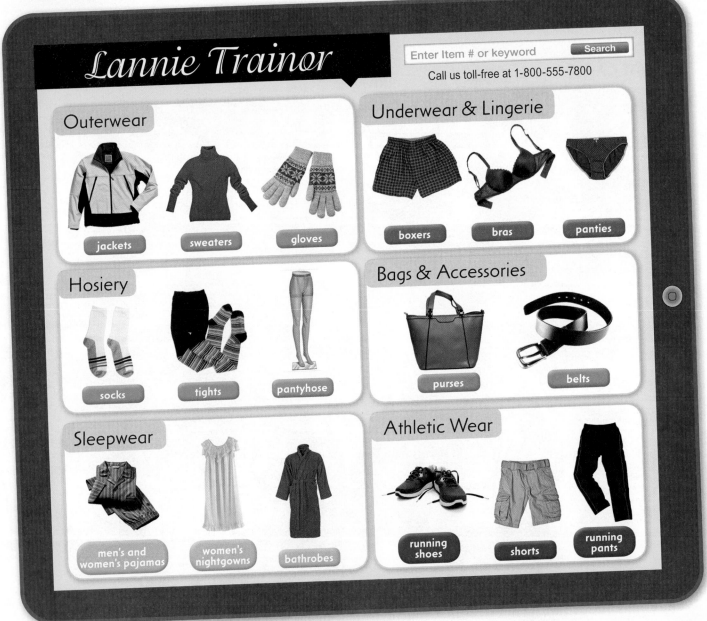

Lannie Trainor

Enter Item # or keyword   Search
Call us toll-free at 1-800-555-7800

Outerwear
jackets   sweaters   gloves

Underwear & Lingerie
boxers   bras   panties

Hosiery
socks   tights   pantyhose

Bags & Accessories
purses   belts

Sleepwear
men's and women's pajamas   women's nightgowns   bathrobes

Athletic Wear
running shoes   shorts   running pants

A ▶4:22 **VOCABULARY** • *Clothes and clothing departments*
Look at the online catalogue. Then listen and repeat.

B **DISCUSSION** What are the advantages and disadvantages of buying clothes online?

    ❝ If you buy clothes online, you don't have to leave home. It's really convenient! ❞

    ❝ But if you don't like something, you have to go to the post office to send it back to the store. That's inconvenient. ❞

C ▶4:23 **PHOTO STORY** Read and listen to a conversation between a clerk and a customer about a sweater the customer wants to buy.

Shopper: Excuse me. How much is that V-neck?

Clerk: This red one? It's $55.

Shopper: That's not too bad. And it's really nice.

Shopper: Could I get it in a larger size?

Clerk: Here you go. This one's a medium. Would you like to try it on?

Shopper: No, thanks. I'll just take it. It's a present for my sister. Would you be nice enough to gift wrap it for me?

Clerk: Of course!

D **THINK AND EXPLAIN** Complete each statement. Then explain your answer.

1 The shopper wants to know the .... of the sweater.

    ⓐ price   **b** size

    How do you know? The shopper says,
    " How much is that V-neck? .... "

2 The shopper asks the clerk for another ....

    a color   **b** size

    How do you know? The shopper says,
    " .... "

3 The clerk brings the shopper a different ....

    a size   **b** color

    How do you know? The clerk says,
    " .... "

4 The sweater is for ....

    a the shopper   **b** a different person

    How do you know? The shopper says,
    " .... "

E **FOCUS ON LANGUAGE** Complete each statement with a quotation from the Photo Story.

1 The shopper says, " .... " to get the clerk's attention.

2 The shopper says, " .... " to say that the price of the sweater is OK.

3 The clerk says, " .... " when she gives the shopper the second sweater.

SPEAKING

DISCUSSION What's important to you when you choose a clothing store or website? Complete the chart. Then compare charts with your classmates. Explain your reasons.

	Not important	Important	Very important
Prices	○	○	○
Brands	○	○	○
Selection	○	○	○
Service	○	○	○

GOAL Shop and pay for clothes

DIGITAL FLASH CARDS

VOCABULARY *Types of clothing and shoes*

Also:
Formal clothes
a dress
a skirt
a suit
a tie

A ▶4:24 Read and listen. Then listen again and repeat.

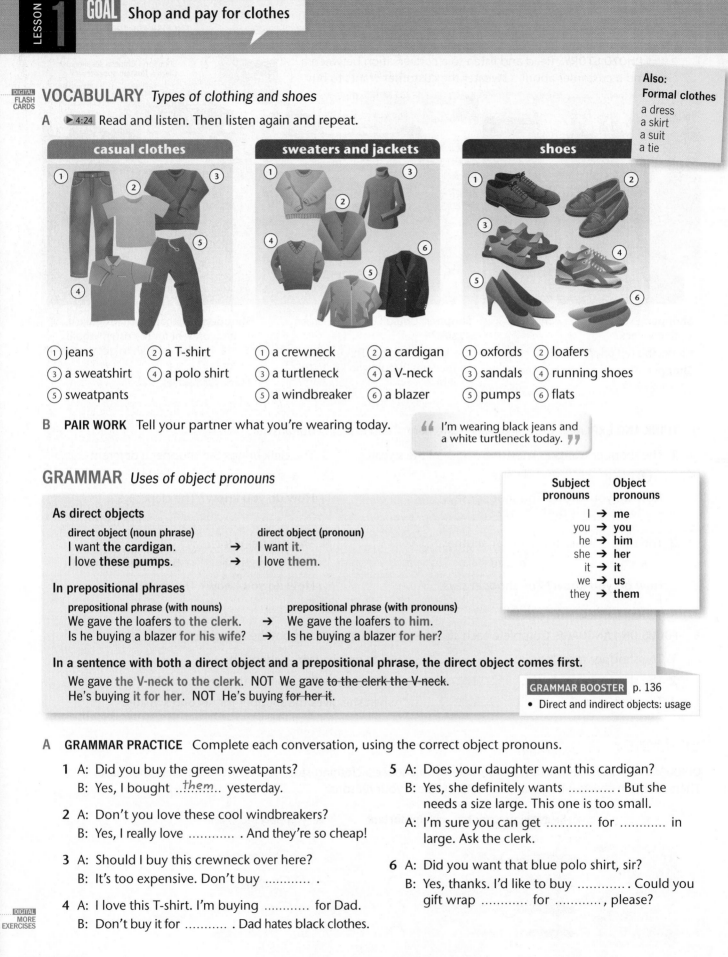

casual clothes

sweaters and jackets

shoes

① jeans ② a T-shirt
③ a sweatshirt ④ a polo shirt
⑤ sweatpants

① a crewneck ② a cardigan
③ a turtleneck ④ a V-neck
⑤ a windbreaker ⑥ a blazer

① oxfords ② loafers
③ sandals ④ running shoes
⑤ pumps ⑥ flats

B **PAIR WORK** Tell your partner what you're wearing today.

❝ I'm wearing black jeans and a white turtleneck today. ❞

GRAMMAR *Uses of object pronouns*

Subject pronouns		Object pronouns
I	→	me
you	→	you
he	→	him
she	→	her
it	→	it
we	→	us
they	→	them

As direct objects

direct object (noun phrase)
I want **the cardigan**. →
I love **these pumps**. →

direct object (pronoun)
I want **it**.
I love **them**.

In prepositional phrases

prepositional phrase (with nouns)
We gave the loafers **to the clerk**. →
Is he buying a blazer **for his wife**? →

prepositional phrase (with pronouns)
We gave the loafers **to him**.
Is he buying a blazer **for her**?

In a sentence with both a direct object and a prepositional phrase, the direct object comes first.

We gave **the V-neck to the clerk**. NOT We gave to the clerk the V-neck.
He's buying **it for her**. NOT He's buying for her it.

GRAMMAR BOOSTER p. 136
• Direct and indirect objects: usage

A **GRAMMAR PRACTICE** Complete each conversation, using the correct object pronouns.

1 A: Did you buy the green sweatpants?
   B: Yes, I bought ...*them*.. yesterday.

2 A: Don't you love these cool windbreakers?
   B: Yes, I really love .... And they're so cheap!

3 A: Should I buy this crewneck over here?
   B: It's too expensive. Don't buy ....

4 A: I love this T-shirt. I'm buying .... for Dad.
   B: Don't buy it for .... Dad hates black clothes.

5 A: Does your daughter want this cardigan?
   B: Yes, she definitely wants .... But she needs a size large. This one is too small.
   A: I'm sure you can get .... for .... in large. Ask the clerk.

6 A: Did you want that blue polo shirt, sir?
   B: Yes, thanks. I'd like to buy .... Could you gift wrap .... for .... , please?

DIGITAL MORE EXERCISES

B GRAMMAR PRACTICE Unscramble the words and phrases to write statements.

1 I / it / for her / buying / am ....

2 getting / they / them / for us / are ....

3 for my son-in-law / I / them / need ....

4 please / it / to me / give ....

5 it / he / is / finding / for me ....

CONVERSATION MODEL

A ▶4:25 Read and listen to someone pay for clothes.

A: I'll take these polo shirts, please.

B: Certainly. How would you like to pay for them?

A: Excuse me?

B: Cash or credit?

A: Credit, please. And could you gift wrap them for me?

B: Of course!

> ▶4:27 **Responses**
> Of course!
> Absolutely!
> Definitely!
> OK.
> Sure.
> Certainly.

B ▶4:26 **RHYTHM AND INTONATION** Listen again and repeat. Then practice the Conversation Model with a partner.

C FIND THE GRAMMAR Find and circle all the object pronouns in the Conversation Model and in the Photo Story on page 87. How many did you find in each place?

NOW YOU CAN Shop and pay for clothes

A CONVERSATION ACTIVATOR Choose clothing from the pictures. (Or choose from the online store on page 86.) Then, with a partner, change the Conversation Model, using the clothes you chose. Use the correct object pronouns. Then change roles.

A: I'll take .... , please.
B: .... How would you like to pay for .... ?
A: Excuse me?
B: Cash or credit?
A: .... , please. And could you gift wrap .... for me?
B: ....

DON'T STOP!

> **Before you pay, talk about other clothes.**
>   I love this / these __!
> **Ask about prices.**
>   How much is / are __?

B CHANGE PARTNERS Create another conversation. Use different clothes

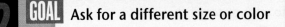

GOAL Ask for a different size or color

VOCABULARY *Clothing that comes in "pairs"*

A ▶4:28 Read and listen. Then listen again and repeat.

(a pair of)
gloves

(a pair of)
pantyhose

(a pair of)
tights

(a pair of)
panties

(a pair of)
pajamas

(a pair of)
shorts

(a pair of)
jeans

(a pair of)
pants

(a pair of)
boxers

(a pair of)
briefs

(a pair of)
socks

(a pair of)
shoes

B ▶4:29 **LISTEN TO INFER** Listen to the conversations. Complete each statement with the name of a clothing department.

1 She should go to ....

2 She should go to ....

3 She got them in ....

4 They're in ....

Departments
Men's underwear
Athletic wear
Outerwear
Lingerie
Sleepwear
Hosiery

GRAMMAR *Comparative adjectives*

Use comparative adjectives to compare two people, places, things, or ideas.

more = ↑
less = ↓

Do you have these pants in a larger size? This pair is a little tight.
I need shoes that are more comfortable. These are very small.
Do you have a pair of less expensive gloves? These are just too expensive.

Use than after the adjective when you compare two people, places, or things.

That suit is nicer than the one I'm wearing.
These gloves are more expensive than the other pair.

The crewneck is nice, but
the cardigan is **nicer**.

▶4:30 **Spelling rules**

+ **er**	+ **r**	+ **ier**	consonant + **er**
small → smaller	large → larger	heavy → heavier	big → bigger
cheap → cheaper	loose → looser	pretty → prettier	hot → hotter

BUT use more or less with adjectives that have two or more syllables and don't end in -y.

more expensive / less comfortable

▶4:31 **Irregular forms**
good → **better**
bad → **worse**

GRAMMAR BOOSTER p. 137
• Comparative adjectives: spelling rules

A GRAMMAR / VOCABULARY PRACTICE Write the opposite of each comparative adjective. More than one correct answer may be possible.

1 smaller ....*larger*........ **3** lighter .... **5** more expensive ....

2 taller .... **4** tighter .... **6** less popular ....

B GRAMMAR PRACTICE Complete each conversation with comparative adjectives. Use <u>than</u> if necessary.

1 A: Don't take that nightgown to Hawaii! It's .... it is here. Take something ....
                                              hot   light
   B: Good idea.

2 A: What do you think of these red gloves?
   B: Beautiful. They're .... the black ones. And they're ...., too.
                                 pretty   cheap

3 A: Excuse me. Do these pants come in a .... length?
                                   long
   B: I'm sure they do. Let me see if I can find you a .... pair.
                                                 good

4 A: I just love these pajamas, but I wish they were ....
                                                warm
   B: Well, these blue ones look warm. Blue is a really flattering color for you, and they're much ....
                                           expensive

DIGITAL
MORE
EXERCISES

CONVERSATION MODEL

A ▶4:32 Read and listen to someone ask for a different size.

   A: Excuse me. Do you have these gloves in a smaller size? I need a medium.

   B: Yes, we do. Here you go.

   A: Thanks.

   B: Would you like to take them?

   A: Yes, please. Thanks for your help.

   B: My pleasure.

Sizes
S	small
M	medium
L	large
XL	extra large
XXL	extra extra large

B ▶4:33 **RHYTHM AND INTONATION** Listen again and repeat. Then practice the Conversation Model with a partner.

NOW YOU CAN Ask for a different size or color

A NOTEPADDING On the notepad, make a list of clothes you'd like to buy.

DIGITAL
VIDEO

B CONVERSATION ACTIVATOR With a partner, personalize the Conversation Model. Use your list of clothes. Ask for a different size or color. Then change roles.

   A: Excuse me. Do you have .... in .... ?
   B: Yes, we do. Here you go.
   A: Thanks.
   B: Would you like to take .... ?
   A: .... Thanks for your help.
   B: ....

I'd like to buy:

DON'T STOP!
• Ask about other clothes, sizes, and colors.
• Pay for the clothes.

RECYCLE THIS LANGUAGE.
Do you have __ in . . .
  a smaller / larger size?
  a darker / lighter color?
  [black]?
  size [10]?
How much is / are __?
How would you like to pay for __?
Cash or credit?

C CHANGE PARTNERS Ask about other types of clothes.

BEFORE YOU LISTEN

▶4:34 **VOCABULARY** • *Interior locations and directions* Read and listen. Then listen again and repeat.

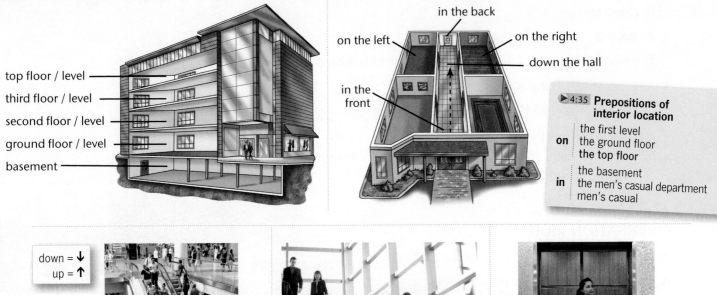

top floor / level
third floor / level
second floor / level
ground floor / level
basement

in the back
on the left
on the right
down the hall
in the front

▶4:35 **Prepositions of interior location**

on
the first level
the ground floor
the top floor

in
the basement
the men's casual department
men's casual

down = ↓
up = ↑

take
go down
go up
the escalator

take
go down
go up
the stairs

take the elevator

LISTENING COMPREHENSION

A ▶4:36 **UNDERSTAND LOCATIONS AND DIRECTIONS** Listen to directions in a department store. Write the number of each location in the white boxes on the floor diagrams.

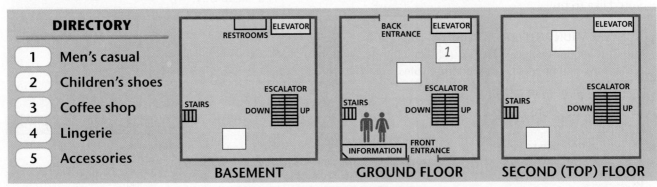

DIRECTORY

1 Men's casual
2 Children's shoes
3 Coffee shop
4 Lingerie
5 Accessories

RESTROOMS ELEVATOR
STAIRS
ESCALATOR
DOWN UP
BASEMENT

BACK ENTRANCE ELEVATOR
1
STAIRS
ESCALATOR
DOWN UP
INFORMATION FRONT ENTRANCE
GROUND FLOOR

ELEVATOR
STAIRS
ESCALATOR
DOWN UP
SECOND (TOP) FLOOR

B **PAIR WORK** Take turns asking for and giving directions to any of the locations.

PRONUNCIATION *Contrastive stress for clarification*

A ▶4:37 Read and listen. Then listen again and repeat.

A: The shoe department is upstairs, on the third floor.

B: Excuse me? The first floor?

A: No. It's on the third floor.

B **PAIR WORK** Now practice the conversation with a partner.

NOW YOU CAN Navigate a mall or department store

A **NOTEPADDING** Choose five departments from the store directory and write one thing you'd like to get in each department.

Department	I'd like . . .
Men's Outerwear	a jacket

Department	I'd like . . .

STORE DIRECTORY

Bags and Accessories	Ground Floor
Electronics	Basement
Hosiery	Ground Floor
Lingerie	Ground Floor
Men's Athletic Wear	2
Men's Casual	2
Men's Outerwear	2
Men's Shoes	2
Men's Sleepwear	2
Men's Underwear	2
Photo Studio	Basement
Restaurant	Basement
Small Appliances	Basement
Women's Casual	Ground Floor
Women's Shoes	Ground Floor

B **REVIEW AND RECYCLE LANGUAGE** Prepare for the role play. Write the four topics below on a separate sheet of paper. With a partner, make a list of language you know for each topic.

1 Ask for directions.

2 Describe store locations.

3 Ask for a size, color, etc.

4 Pay for things.

1	Ask for directions
	Excuse me. I'm looking for the hosiery
	department.

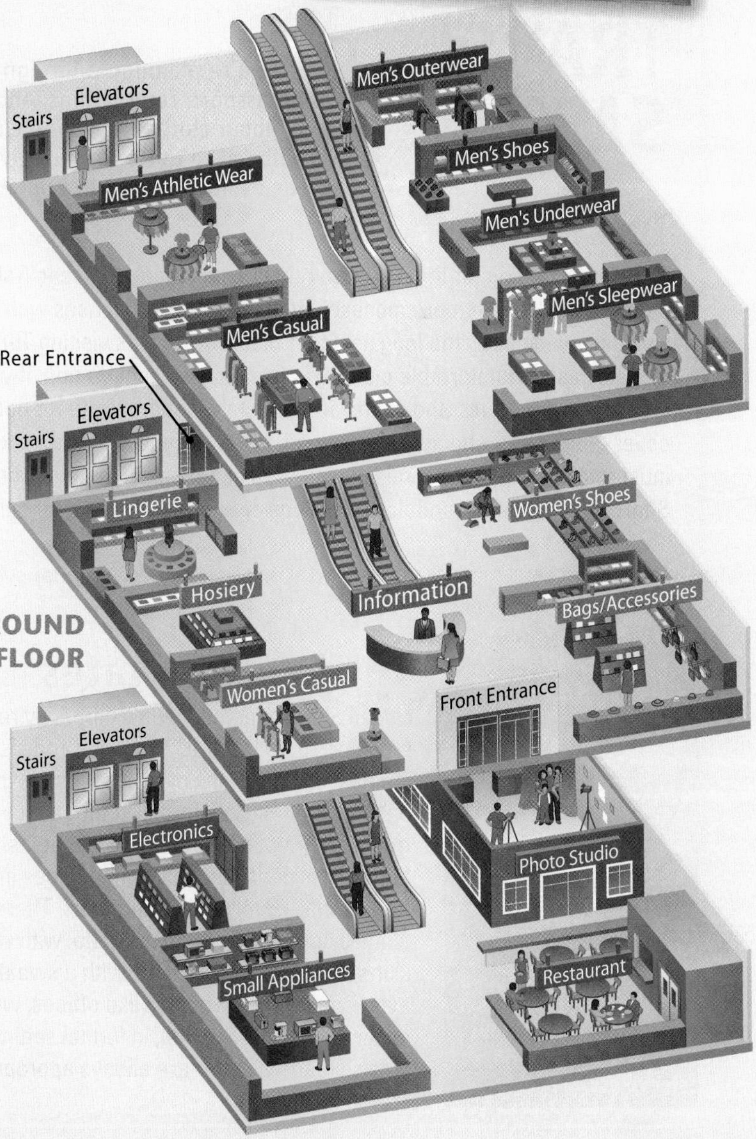

C **ROLE PLAY** Using the floor plan, role-play a conversation between the shopper and the clerk at the information desk. Use your notepad from Exercise A. Use your vocabulary lists from Exercise B. Then change partners, roles, and items you'd like to buy.

" Excuse me. I'm looking for . . . "

GOAL Discuss clothing do's and don'ts

BEFORE YOU READ

▶4:38 **VOCABULARY** • *Formality and appropriateness* Read and listen to each pair of antonyms. Then listen again and repeat.

DIGITAL FLASH CARDS

Formality	Appropriateness	Strictness
formal for special events when casual clothes are not OK	**appropriate** socially correct	**liberal** without many rules for appropriate dress
informal for everyday events when casual clothes are OK	**inappropriate** socially incorrect	**conservative** with more rules for appropriate dress

READING ▶4:39

| Last-Minute Travel Deals | Packing Tips | Cultural Information | Health and Safety | About Us |

TRAVEL SMART

{ OK. You're planning a foreign trip. After you get your passport, reservations, and tickets, it's time to think about clothes. Clothing customs can vary from very liberal to quite conservative. Compare clothing do's and don'ts in two popular destinations. }

Istanbul: the Blue Mosque

Turkey

Pack light clothing for the heat. Even though most tourists wear T-shirts and shorts, Turkish people usually wear more modest clothes: dresses or blouses with sleeves for women, and short-sleeved shirts and long pants for men. For tourists visiting Turkey's beautiful historic places, casual comfortable clothing is fine for men and women. If you visit a mosque, however, the dress code is stricter, and shorts are definitely inappropriate for both men and women. Women must cover their knees, shoulders, and head, and men must cover their knees and shoulders. Everyone must remove his or her shoes. On Turkey's beaches, on the other hand, anything goes for tourists. Shorts, T-shirts, and sandals or flip-flops are normal for both Turkish people and foreigners.

Flip-flops are popular summer shoes almost everywhere.

In some countries, people consider sleeveless blouses inappropriate. However in the U.S., it's always OK for women to go sleeveless.

The United States

United States weather in July differs by region. A good rule of thumb is to check an Internet weather site to be sure. The dress code is generally liberal, so it's common in the warmer months for Americans of both sexes to wear T-shirts, shorts, and sandals or flip-flops on the street and in informal settings. But young people frequently wear some pretty wild clothes! The dress code, however, is definitely *not* anything goes in schools, formal restaurants, or religious institutions. There, more conservative clothes and shoes are appropriate, with women wearing skirts, dresses, or nice pants with a sweater or a blouse. But even in more formal places like offices, women never have to cover their arms. For men, in formal settings, a suit and tie or a nice shirt and a blazer are always appropriate.

In the U.S., young people's style is often "anything goes."

A **IDENTIFY SUPPORTING DETAILS** Circle T (<u>true</u>) or F (<u>false</u>). Explain each of your responses.

T F **1** It's appropriate to wear shorts in Turkish mosques.

T F **2** The dress code for tourists is pretty liberal on Turkish beaches.

T F **3** Clothing customs in Turkey are "anything goes" for everyone.

T F **4** The United States is very conservative about clothes.

T F **5** It's appropriate for young Americans to wear wild clothes in religious institutions.

T F **6** Flip-flops are inappropriate in formal restaurants in the United States.

B **PARAPHRASE** What are the main differences in the dress codes of Turkey and the United States? Use the Vocabulary from page 94 in your description.

C **APPLY INFORMATION** Imagine you are going on a trip to New York in June, when the weather is warm or hot during the day and cool at night. You want to go to nice restaurants and visit historic places and parks. Plan your clothes for a one-week visit. Be specific. Explain your choices.

DIGITAL
MORE
EXERCISES

> " I'm taking two or three pairs of shorts. It's really warm in the summer there, and it's OK to wear casual clothes in New York. . . . "

NOW YOU CAN Discuss clothing do's and don'ts

A **FRAME YOUR IDEAS** Take the opinion survey.

What's Your Personal Dress Code?

Check <u>agree</u> or <u>disagree</u>.	agree	disagree
It's appropriate for men to wear shorts on the street.	◯	◯
It's inappropriate for women to wear shorts on the street.	◯	◯
It's appropriate for men to wear sandals in an office.	◯	◯
It's important for men to wear ties in an office.	◯	◯
It's inappropriate for men to wear sleeveless T-shirts in a restaurant.	◯	◯
It's appropriate for women to wear short skirts or shorts in a religious institution.	◯	◯

How Would You Rate Yourself?

◯ Conservative   ◯ Liberal   ◯ "Anything Goes!"

B **NOTEPADDING** With a partner, write some clothing do's and don'ts for visitors to your country. Do the same rules apply to both men and women? Use the survey as a guide.

in offices:

in formal restaurants:

in casual social settings:

in religious institutions:

C **GROUP WORK** Now discuss clothing do's and don'ts for your country. Does everyone agree?

> **Text-mining (optional)**
> Find and underline three words or phrases in the Reading that were new to you. Use them in your Group Work.
>   For example: "modest clothes."

A ▶4:40 Listen to the conversations. Use the context to infer which department the people are in. Listen more than once if necessary.

1 ....
2 ....
3 ....
4 ....
5 ....

Departments
Shoes
Bags and Accessories
Hosiery
Outerwear
Sleepwear
Lingerie
Electronics

B Express your opinion. Complete the chart with the appropriate kinds of shoes and clothes for certain places and occasions.

	Shoes	Clothes
To class or work		
On formal occasions		
On the weekend		

C Complete the travel article with the comparative form of each adjective. Use <u>than</u> when necessary.

Travel & Clothing

When you travel, think carefully about the clothes you pack. As far as color is concerned, ... colors are usually .... For ....
   1 dark   2 practical   3 cool

destinations, a blazer can be .... a windbreaker or
                                    4 convenient

cardigan because you can wear it in .... settings such as offices
                                  5 conservative

and .... restaurants. For travel to .... areas of the world,
        6 formal   7 hot

.... clothes are .... ones.
  8 light   9 comfortable   10 heavy

D Rewrite each sentence. Change the underlined prepositional and noun phrases to object pronouns.

1 Please show <u>the loafers to my husband</u>. *Please show them to him.* ....

2 They sent <u>the jeans to their grandchildren</u>. ....

3 How is she paying <u>Robert for the clothes</u>? ....

4 When are we buying <u>the gift for Marie</u>? ....

WRITING

Imagine that you have a friend from another country who is coming to visit you in January. Write a letter or e-mail to your friend, explaining what to pack for the trip. Give your friend advice on appropriate and inappropriate dress.

Hi! Here are some clothing tips for your visit. First of all, the "rules" here are . . .

For additional language practice . . .

♫ TOP NOTCH **POP** • Lyrics p. 150
"Anything Goes"

DIGITAL SONG   DIGITAL KARAOKE

WRITING BOOSTER p. 146
• Connecting ideas with <u>because</u> and <u>since</u>
• Guidance for this writing exercise

ORAL REVIEW

CONTEST Study the picture. Name all the kinds of sweaters and shoes and the kinds of clothing that come in pairs. (The student who can name the most kinds wins.)

PAIR WORK With a partner, make comparisons about the clothes. For example:

Blazers are more formal than windbreakers.

ROLE PLAY Look at the directory. Create conversations for the following people:
* the shoppers and clerks at the information desk
* the customer and the clerk talking about the jackets
* the clerk and the customer paying for clothes

GIFT WRAPPING ↗

DIRECTORY

BAGS AND ACCESSORIES	1
CHILDREN'S DEPARTMENT	3
ELECTRONICS	3
HAIRDRESSER	4
LINGERIE	1
MEN'S DEPARTMENT	1
PHOTO STUDIO	2
RESTAURANTS	4
SHOES	1
TRAVEL AGENCY	2
WOMEN'S DEPARTMENT	1

INFORMATION

FITTING ROOM →

$

$$$

LARGE

MEDIUM

✓ NOW I CAN

☐ Shop and pay for clothes.
☐ Ask for a different size or color.
☐ Navigate a mall or department store.
☐ Discuss clothing do's and don'ts.

Taking Transportation

COMMUNICATION GOALS

1 Discuss schedules and buy tickets.
2 Book travel services.
3 Understand airport announcements.
4 Describe transportation problems.

PREVIEW

BUSES FROM LIMA TO NAZCA

DESTINATION	FREQUENCY	DEPARTURE	ARRIVAL	STOPS	BUS TERMINAL
Nazca	Daily	04:30	10:45	Paracas	Terminal Nazca
Nazca	Daily	07:00	13:30	Paracas-Ica	Terminal Nazca
Nazca	Daily	13:30	20:00	Paracas-Ica	Terminal Nazca
Nazca	Daily	14:00	20:00	Non-stop	Terminal Nazca
Nazca	Daily	17:30	23:30	Non-stop	Terminal Nazca

BEIJING to SHANGHAI

Train No.	Depart	Arrive	Travel Time	Air conditioning
D31	11:05	20:49	0d 09h 44m	✓
1461	14:42	12:49	0d 22h 07m	✗
Z21	19:32	07:00	0d 11h 28m	✓
Z13	19:38	07:06	0d 11h 28m	✓
Z7	19:44	07:12	0d 11h 28m	✓

OSAKA (Itami) to TOKYO (Haneda)

Flight No.	Departure	Arrival	Frequency	Aircraft Type
22	07:10	08:15	DAILY	ER10
4	07:30	08:35	DAILY	ER10
26	08:30	09:35	DAILY	ER10
30	10:30	11:35	DAILY	ER10
34	11:30	12:35	DAILY	ER10

A Read the schedules. Use them to find the answers to the questions.

1 It's now 10:00 A.M. When is the next bus to Nazca?

2 When is the next non-stop bus to Nazca?

3 How much time does it take to get from Beijing to Shanghai on train 1461?

4 Which train is faster, train 1461 or train D31?

5 What time does flight 26 depart for Tokyo? When does it arrive?

B **PAIR WORK** Ask your partner more questions about each schedule.

> " How long is the flight from Osaka to Tokyo? "

C ▶5:02 **PHOTO STORY** Read and listen to a conversation between two people trying to catch a flight.

ENGLISH FOR TODAY'S WORLD
Understand English speakers from different language backgrounds.
Marcos = Portuguese speaker
Roger = French speaker

Marcos: Excuse me. Do you speak English?
Roger: Actually I'm French. But, yes.
Marcos: Thank goodness! I'm looking for Terminal 2.
Roger: No problem. I'm on my way there now. Just follow me.

Roger: So where are you flying today?
Marcos: Manila. Then I'm connecting to a flight home.
Roger: Well, that's a coincidence. I'm catching a flight to Manila, too. Flight 56?
Marcos: Yes. But we should hurry. The plane's boarding in fifteen minutes.

Roger: And where is home?
Marcos: Brazil. São Paulo.
Roger: No kidding! I'm going to go to São Paulo next week!
Marcos: Really? What a small world!

D **FOCUS ON LANGUAGE** Find and write an underlined word or expression from the Photo Story with the same meaning:

1 I'm taking a plane to . . .   **2** Let's walk faster.   **3** I'm taking another flight to . . .

....

E **THINK AND EXPLAIN** Circle T (true), F (false), or NI (no information). Then explain each answer.

T F NI **1** Flight 56 leaves from Terminal 2.   T F NI **4** Marcos is staying in Manila.

T F NI **2** Roger lives in France.   T F NI **5** Roger is staying in Manila.

T F NI **3** Roger and Marcos are both flying to Manila.   T F NI **6** The two men get to the flight on time.

SPEAKING

PAIR WORK Complete the chart with the means of transportation you prefer for each occasion. Then discuss your choices with a partner.

RECYCLE THIS LANGUAGE.

popular	cheap
convenient	scenic
affordable	boring
comfortable	long
expensive	short
relaxing	scary

| To school or work | bus | affordable, convenient, I can read or work. |

	Means of transportation	Reason
To school or work		
To social events on weekends		
For travel in my country		
For travel outside of my country		

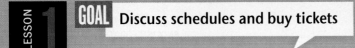

LESSON 1

GOAL Discuss schedules and buy tickets

VOCABULARY *Kinds of tickets and trips*

A ▶5:03 Read and listen. Then listen again and repeat.

JAPAN RAIL	Kodama (local)	Nozomi (express)
Tokyo	10:13	10:20
Odawara	10:30	–
Atami	11:00	–
Maibara	13:39	–
Kyoto	14:04	12:38

PASSENGER TICKET
KOREA BUS LINE
SEOUL > SOKCHO

a one-way ticket

PASSENGER TICKET
KOREA BUS LINE
SEOUL > SOKCHO
SOKCHO > SEOUL

a round-trip ticket

the local   the express

Air China
Flight
009
New York → Los Angeles → Taipei

a direct flight

Air China
Flight
808
New York → Taipei

a non-stop flight

an aisle seat   a window seat

B Complete the conversations with phrases from the Vocabulary.

1 A: Would you like a window or an aisle?

B: .... I like to walk around.

2 A: Is Flight 3 a .... flight?

B: No. It's a .... flight. It makes a stop, but you don't have to change planes.

3 A: Do you want a .... ticket to Rome?

B: Actually, I need a .... I'm not coming back!

4 A: I'm sorry. It's too late to make the ....

B: Well, I'll take the .... I'm not in a hurry.

GRAMMAR *Modals should and could*

should

Use should and the base form of a verb to give advice or to make a strong suggestion.

You **shouldn't take** that flight. You **should take** the non-stop.
Should they **take** the bus? (Yes, they should. / No, they shouldn't.)
When **should** we **leave**? (Before 2:00.)

could

Use could and the base form of a verb to offer alternatives or to make a weak suggestion.

The express bus is full, but you **could take** the local.
Could I **take** the 2:20? (Yes, you could. / No, you couldn't.)

GRAMMAR BOOSTER p. 138
• Modals can, could, and should: meaning, form, and common errors

A **GRAMMAR PRACTICE** Complete each statement or question with a form of *should* or *could* and the base form.

1 .... the express. The local arrives too late.
   he / take

2 They said .... two aisle seats or an aisle and a window seat.
   we / have

3 .... a one-way ticket. It's much more expensive each way.
      <u>you / not get</u>

4 Which train ....? We absolutely have to be there on time.
      <u>we / take</u>

5 .... a ticket at the station or on the train. It doesn't matter.
      <u>they / buy</u>

B PAIR WORK Two co-workers are at Penn Station, and they work in Oak Plains. It's 7:20 A.M. They have to arrive in Oak Plains for work at 9:00. Use the schedule to discuss all the possible choices. Use <u>could</u> and <u>should</u>. Explain your choices.

Blue numbers = express trains

Penn Station	Northway	Oak Plains	Carmel
7:15	7:50	8:30	9:00
7:25	-----	8:25	8:55
7:30	-----	-----	8:55
7:30	8:05	8:45	9:15
7:50	8:25	9:05	9:35

    ❝ They could take the 7:30 express. ❞

        ❝ No. That train doesn't stop in Oak Plains. ❞

CONVERSATION MODEL

A ▶5:04 Read and listen to someone buy tickets.

A: Can I still make the 5:12 bus to Montreal?

B: I'm sorry. It left five minutes ago.

A: <u>Too bad</u>. What should I do?

B: Well, you could take the 5:30.

A: OK. One ticket, please.

B: One-way or round-trip?

A: Round-trip, please.

▶5:06 **Ways to express disappointment**
Too bad.
What a shame.
Oh, no!

B ▶5:05 **RHYTHM AND INTONATION** Listen again and repeat. Then practice the Conversation Model with a partner.

NOW YOU CAN Discuss schedules and buy tickets

A CONVERSATION ACTIVATOR Choose a place on the train departure board. Imagine it is now 7:15. With a partner, change the Conversation Model, based on where you want to go. Express disappointment. Then change roles.

A: Can I still make the .... train to .... ?

B: No, I'm sorry. It left .... minutes ago.

A: .... What should I do?

B: Well, you could take the ....

A: OK. One ticket, please.

B: One-way or round-trip?

A: .... , please.

DON'T STOP!
• Discuss the price of tickets.
• Ask whether the train is a local or an express.
• Ask for the kind of seat you'd like.

```
DEPARTURES  07:15 AM

TO                DEPARTS   TRACK
WASHINGTON        06:55         6
BALTIMORE         07:03         9
NEWARK            07:12        19
WASHINGTON        08:23         8
BALTIMORE         08:26         9
NEWARK            08:31        18
```

B CHANGE PARTNERS Practice the conversation again, using the bus, train, and flight schedules on page 98. Discuss other departures.

GOAL Book travel services

GRAMMAR *Be going to* + base form to express the future: Review

I'm going to take the bus to New York. I'm not going to fly.
She's going to eat at the airport. She's not (or She isn't) going to eat at home.
We're going to take a taxi into town. We're not (or We aren't) going to drive.

Remember: The present continuous is also often used to express future plans.
Next week, **I'm taking** the bus to New York.

Questions

Are they **going to need** a taxi? (Yes, they are. / No, they aren't.)
Is Beth **going to make** a reservation? (Yes, she is. / No, she isn't.)

When **are** you **going to arrive**? (At noon.) Who **are** they **going to meet**? (The travel agent.)
Where **is** he **going to wait**? (In the restaurant.) Who's **going to take** me to the airport? (Tom is.)

GRAMMAR BOOSTER p. 139
• Expansion: future actions

A GRAMMAR PRACTICE Complete each statement or question with <u>be going to</u> and the base form of the verb.

1 .... tickets for
the express.   they / not buy

4 Who .... him to
the train station?   take

2 When .... for
the airport?   she / leave

5 Who .... in
Chicago?   he / call

3 .... an aisle seat?
you / ask for

6 Where .... when I arrive?
Dad / be

B Complete the e-mail. Circle the correct verb forms.

Here's my travel information: I (1 go to leaving / 'm going to leave) Mexico City at 4:45 P.M. on Atlas Airlines
flight 6702, and I'm arriving in Chicago at 9:50 P.M. Mara's flight (2 is going to get there / going to get there)
ten minutes later, so we (3 're go meeting / 're going to meet) at the taxi stand downstairs. That's too
late for you to come to the airport, so we can take the express bus from O'Hare to the city. Mara
(4 goes to spend / is going to spend) the night at our apartment. Her flight to Tokyo isn't leaving until
the next day, and she and I (5 are going to spend / going to spend) the whole day shopping!

C PAIR WORK Ask your partner three questions about
his or her future plans. Use <u>be going to</u>.

❝ What are you going to
do on your next trip? ❞

VOCABULARY *Travel services*

A ▶5:07 Read and listen. Then listen again and repeat.

a rental car

a taxi

a limousine / a limo

a hotel reservation

B ▶5:08 **LISTEN TO INFER** Listen to the conversations. Then listen again and complete each sentence with <u>be going to</u> and infer the name of a travel service.

1 He .... (reserve)
.... for her.

2 The tourist .... (need)
.... in Seoul.

3 She .... (get)
.... at John F. Kennedy Airport.

4 The agent .... (check) to
see if he can reserve .... for the tourist.

CONVERSATION MODEL

A ▶5:09 Read and listen to a conversation between a travel agent and a business traveler.

A: Hello. Baker Travel. Can I help you?

B: I hope so. I'm going to need a car in Dubai.

A: Certainly. What date are you arriving?

B: April 6ᵗʰ.

A: And what time?

B: Let me check . . . 5:45 P.M.

B ▶5:10 **RHYTHM AND INTONATION** Listen again and repeat. Then practice the Conversation Model with a partner.

C **FIND THE GRAMMAR** Find and underline two ways that A and B express future plans in the Conversation Model.

NOW YOU CAN Book travel services

PASSENGER TICKET AND BAGGAGE CHECK
AIR CUZCO APRIL 11 FLIGHT 22
DEPARTURE: 18:00   ARRIVAL: 19:15
LIMA TO CUZCO
88985376124   0 988 7631986534 7

DIGITAL VIDEO COACH

A **CONVERSATION ACTIVATOR** With a partner, change the Conversation Model. Book a rental car, a taxi, or a limousine. Use the tickets for arrival information. Then change roles.

A: Hello. Can I help you?

B: I hope so. I'm going to need ....
in ....

A: .... What date are you arriving?

B: ....

A: And what time?

B: Let me check . . . .

DON'T STOP!

Book additional services.
I'm also going to need
[a hotel reservation].

Seoul Touristbus
FROM Seoul
TO Sokcho
DATE 13 August
DEPARTS 07:45
ARRIVES 11:55

B **CHANGE PARTNERS** Make your own flight, bus, or train ticket. Then practice the conversation again, using <u>your</u> ticket.

Your Ticket

From

To

Date

Departs   Arrives

BOARDING PASS
EXCELA RAIL TRANSPORT
JUNE 26 EXPRESS TRAIN
NEW YORK TO WASHINGTON
DEPARTURE: 6:00 PM
ARRIVAL: 9:10 PM

GOAL **Understand airport announcements**

BEFORE YOU LISTEN

DIGITAL FLASH CARDS

A ▶5:11 **VOCABULARY •** *Airline passenger information* Read and listen. Then listen again and repeat.

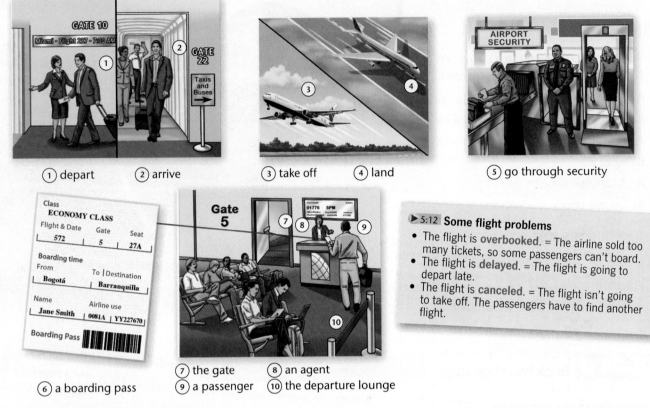

① depart ② arrive ③ take off ④ land ⑤ go through security

⑥ a boarding pass ⑦ the gate ⑧ an agent ⑨ a passenger ⑩ the departure lounge

▶5:12 **Some flight problems**

- The flight is **overbooked**. = The airline sold too many tickets, so some passengers can't board.
- The flight is **delayed**. = The flight is going to depart late.
- The flight is **canceled**. = The flight isn't going to take off. The passengers have to find another flight.

B Use the Vocabulary to complete the pre-flight instructions.

Rapid Air pre-flight instructions

When you .... at the airport, you should take your luggage to the check-in
counter and get your .... Then you can .... ,
where .... have to put all their hand luggage on the belt. From there
you should go to the .... your plane is departing from. If you are early
and your plane isn't at the gate, just have a seat in the ....
When they call your flight, you can show your boarding pass to the ....
and get on the plane. Be sure to turn off your phone before your plane ....
from the gate. Enjoy the takeoff, and have a good flight!

LISTENING COMPREHENSION

A ▶5:13 **LISTEN FOR DETAILS** Listen to the announcements.
Write the flight information.

1 flight number: ....
2 original departure gate: ....
3 final departure gate: ....
4 final departure time: ....

B ▶5:14 **LISTEN TO UNDERSTAND ANNOUNCEMENTS** Listen again and check the travel problems.

☐ a delay ☐ a gate change

☐ a cancellation ☐ a security problem

☐ an overbooked flight ☐ a mechanical problem

PRONUNCIATION *Intonation for offering alternatives*

A ▶5:15 Listen to the rhythm and intonation of alternatives. Then listen again and repeat.

1 Well, you could take the train or the bus.

2 They could wait or reserve a later flight.

3 Would you like one-way or round-trip?

B Now practice saying each sentence on your own.

NOW YOU CAN Understand airport announcements

A ▶5:16 Read and listen to the announcement by the gate agent. Make sure you understand the details.

> " Good afternoon, ladies and gentlemen. Rapid Air Flight 58 from Brasília to São Paulo is overbooked. We apologize. We need two volunteers to give up their seats on this flight. There are seats available on all later flights to São Paulo. If you volunteer to take a later flight, Rapid Air will give you a free round-trip ticket anywhere we fly. The free ticket is good for one year. "

B **PAIR WORK** Imagine that you and your partner are business travelers. You have tickets on flight 58. Here is the situation:

• The time is now 16:35.

• You're on your way to an important dinner in São Paulo at 20:30.

• The flight takes about two hours gate to gate.

Look at the departure schedule and discuss your alternatives.

DEPARTURES			
São Paulo	56	16:20	departed
Rio de Janeiro	89	16:40	boarding
São Paulo	58	16:50	now 17:25
São Paulo	60	17:50	on time

C **DISCUSSION** Summarize your decision for the class and explain why you made that decision. How many students decided to take a later flight?

We could volunteer. Flight 60 is going to arrive before the dinner. What do you think?

I don't know. I think we should stay on flight 58. There's always a lot of traffic in São Paulo. We can't be late for the dinner.

GOAL Describe transportation problems

BEFORE YOU READ

A ▶ 5:17 **VOCABULARY** • *Transportation problems* Read and listen. Then listen again and repeat.

We **had an accident.**

We **had mechanical problems.**

We **missed** our **train.**

We **got bumped from the flight.**

We **got seasick.**

Also:
carsick 🚗
airsick ✈️

B ▶ 5:18 **LISTEN TO ACTIVATE VOCABULARY** Listen and complete each statement with the Vocabulary.

1 They ....
2 They ....
3 They ....
4 They ....
5 They ....

READING ▶ 5:19

GOT BUMPED FROM A FLIGHT?
Maybe it's not so bad after all . . .

As most travelers know, airlines commonly overbook flights because of the large and predictable number of "no-shows"—people who have reservations but don't show up for the flight. Overbooking helps airlines limit the number of empty seats on their flights. However, if a flight is overbooked, some passengers with confirmed reservations have to get off the plane.

Getting bumped isn't always a bad thing, however. There is a growing number of passengers who feel lucky if their flight is overbooked. Why? Because airlines have to provide bumped passengers with cash, free flights, hotels, and/or meals to compensate them for their inconvenience.

In fact, airlines usually ask for volunteers to get off an overbooked flight in exchange for those perks, and many passengers say "Sure!" and happily deplane. Some people even make a habit of choosing flights that are likely to be overbooked, just so they can volunteer!

Driver blames GPS for train crash

BEDFORD HILLS–Last night, Edward Carter, 43, of White Plains told police that his car's global positioning system (GPS) instructed him to make a wrong turn directly onto the train tracks in Bedford Hills. When he turned, his car became stuck on the track, and he had to abandon the car.

In a statement to the police, the man said he was driving north with his son on the Saw Mill Parkway at about 8 P.M. They planned to go to a restaurant on Route 117.

The location of last night's accident

Following the instructions from his GPS unit, he exited the parkway at Green Lane. But then, instead of driving to Route 117 and turning right there, he made a very wrong turn. He turned right at the railroad tracks. The man and his son tried to move the car off the tracks, but they couldn't. Shortly afterward, a Metro-North commuter train hit Mr. Carter's car. Luckily, there were no deaths or injuries. Police say that drivers need to pay attention to the road, not the GPS unit.

CRITICAL THINKING   Based on the Reading and your own ideas, discuss the following topics.

  1 Why do you think airlines overbook flights?

  2 Are there some advantages of getting bumped from a flight? What are they?

  3 What are some advantages of GPS systems? What are some disadvantages?

  4 Do you prefer GPS systems, online maps with instructions, or paper maps? Explain.

DIGITAL
MORE
EXERCISES

NOW YOU CAN   Describe transportation problems

A   Check all the means of transportation you have taken. Then add other means you know.

  ☐ bus   ☐ train   ☐ taxi   ☐ limousine   ☐ ferry

  ☐ ship   ☐ airplane   ☐ helicopter   ☐ other ....

B   **PAIR WORK**   Ask your partner questions about the means of transportation he or she checked.

> ❝ When was the last time you took a train? ❞

C   **NOTEPADDING**   Choose a time when you had transportation problems. On the notepad, make notes about the trip.

means of transportation:
month, day, or year of trip:
destination:
problems:

D   **GROUP WORK**   Now tell your story to your classmates. Describe your transportation problems. Ask them questions about their problems.

> You won't believe what happened on my business trip. First, I got carsick in the airport limo. Then . . .

Text-mining (optional)
Find and underline three words or phrases in the Reading that were new to you. Use them in your Group Work.
For example: "no-shows."

RECYCLE THIS LANGUAGE.

Problems		Responses
The __ was terrible.	Someone stole my __.	What was wrong with the __?
The __ were unfriendly.	The __ drove me crazy.	I'm sorry to hear that.
They canceled my __.	The [flight] was bumpy / scary.	That's a shame / too bad.
The __ didn't work.	The [drive] was long / boring.	Oh, no!
They lost my __.		

REVIEW

A ▶5:20 It's 7:26 A.M. now. Listen as you look at the departure board. Then listen again and use reasoning to determine if each statement is true or false. Circle T (<u>true</u>) or F (<u>false</u>).

DEPARTURES		7:26 A.M.
TO	**DEPARTS**	**TRACK**
WASHINGTON	7:10	6
BOSTON	7:22	9
PHILADELPHIA	7:25	19
WASHINGTON	8:25	8
BOSTON	8:26	24
PHILADELPHIA	8:31	18

T F **1** They could take the 8:31.

T F **2** They should take the 8:25.

T F **3** They're going to Boston.

T F **4** They're both going to take the train to Washington.

T F **5** He usually takes the 7:25.

T F **6** They should hurry.

B Complete each statement with a correct word or phrase.

1 It's important to make a .... early because it can be difficult to find a room after you arrive.

2 When your whole family is going to the airport together, you can reserve a .... It's usually very comfortable and has space for all of your luggage.

3 It can be convenient to book a .... if you want to drive but can't bring your own car.

4 Do you think I could take the .... train? I know it's much faster, but I'm not sure it stops at my station on weekends.

5 My husband always gets an .... seat. He likes to get up and walk around on long flights.

6 I hope it's a .... flight. I get really scared every time the plane takes off or lands.

7 It's not a non-stop, but it's a .... flight. You don't have to change planes, but the plane stops twice.

8 Are you kidding? The flight was .... ? That was the last flight! Just ten minutes ago they said it was here and ready to board!

9 The airline .... the flight, and when I got to the gate, the agent said another passenger had my seat. I had such bad luck!

C Complete the conversation with <u>be going to</u> and the indicated verbs.

A: On Saturday, ... for Cancún.

                                  1 we / leave

B: Really? .... a rental car there? There are some

                            2 you / book

great places to explore.

A: No. I think .... on the beach and rest.

                           3 we / stay

By the way, where .... for your vacation?

                        4 you and Margo / go

B: I'm not sure. But .... to Bangkok on

                        5 I / travel

business next month, and .... a few days

                        6 I / take

off to go sightseeing. I hear it's great.

For additional language practice . . .

♫ TOP NOTCH **POP** • Lyrics p. 150
"Five Hundred Ways"

DIGITAL SONG   DIGITAL KARAOKE

WRITING

Write two paragraphs—one about your most recent trip and one about your next trip. In the first paragraph, describe the transportation you took and write about any problems you had. In the second paragraph, write about the transportation you plan to take. Use <u>be going to</u>.

WRITING BOOSTER p. 147
• The paragraph
• Guidance for this writing exercise

ORAL REVIEW

CONTEST Form teams. Create questions about the pictures to ask another team. (Teams get one point for each correct question and one point for each correct answer.)

What day are they going to take the trip?

ROLE PLAY Choose one picture. Create a conversation for the people. Use <u>could</u> and <u>should</u>. For example:

Agent: You could go to Hawaii or . . .

GROUP STORY Take turns telling the story in the pictures. Each student adds one sentence.

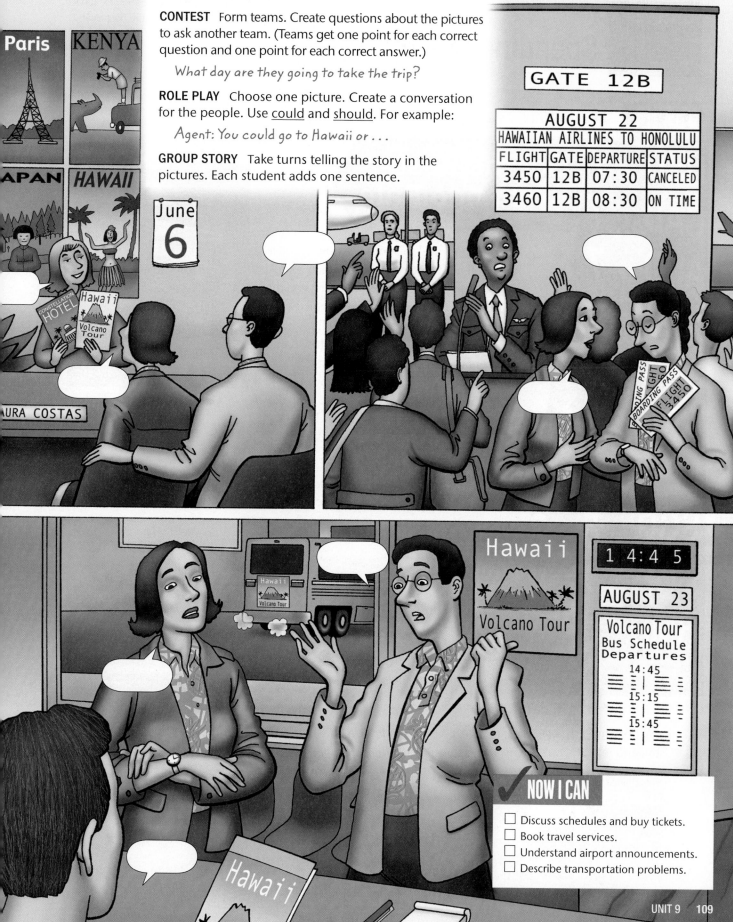

✓ NOW I CAN

- ☐ Discuss schedules and buy tickets.
- ☐ Book travel services.
- ☐ Understand airport announcements.
- ☐ Describe transportation problems.

UNIT 10 Spending Money

COMMUNICATION GOALS

1 Ask for a recommendation.
2 Bargain for a lower price.
3 Discuss showing appreciation for service.
4 Describe where to get the best deals.

PREVIEW

USD 7
CAD 7
AUD 7.
NZD 5.
JPY 0.
GBP 11
EUR 9.7
SGD 5.3
CHF 7.8
RMB 0.9

Check foreign exchange rates before you travel.

Get the Best Exchange Rate

Before you travel to another country, check the **exchange rate** of your currency against the currency of the foreign country you're visiting. If you have to exchange **cash** during your trip, there are usually better rates at banks and post offices. However, you'll get the best rate if you just get **foreign currency** at an **ATM**. But check with your bank before you leave to make sure you can use your ATM card in the country you are visiting.

When possible, use a credit card for larger expenses such as hotel bills, tickets, and car rentals. But be careful—check first to see if your credit card company or bank adds a **fee** for these transactions.

Exchange rates are usually lower at an ATM.

VISTAcard — Monthly Statement

Date	Transaction	Debit
10/07	CAFÉ LUNA	200.00
10/06	*FOREIGN TRANSACTION FEE	4.68
10/06	HOTEL DE CALLAO	180.00

A ▶5:23 **VOCABULARY** • *Financial terms*
Listen and repeat.

> an exchange rate
> cash
> foreign currency
> an ATM
> a fee

B **PAIR WORK** Ask and answer the questions.

1 Do you—or does anyone you know—ever exchange money for foreign currency? When? How?

2 When do people generally use cash? When do they usually use credit cards?

C ▶5:24 **PHOTO STORY** Read and listen to people shop for souvenirs.

ENGLISH FOR TODAY'S WORLD
Understand English speakers from different language backgrounds.
Clerk = Italian speaker

Jenn: Oh, no. I'm almost out of cash. And I want to get a gift for my mom. I sure hope these shops accept credit cards.

Pat: I'll bet they do. Let's go in here. They have some really nice stuff. And I want to get some souvenirs of our trip.

Jenn: Great!

Pat: Hey, what do you think of this?

Jenn: It's gorgeous. But it's a bit more than I want to spend.

Pat: Maybe you can get a better price. It can't hurt to ask.

Jenn: I don't know. I'm not very good at bargaining.

Clerk: Excuse me. Maybe I can help. Let me show you something more affordable.

Jenn: Oh, that one's nice, too. How much do you want for it?

Clerk: Forty euros.

Jenn: I'll take it. You do accept credit cards, don't you?

Clerk: Sorry, no. But there is an ATM right across the street.

D **FOCUS ON LANGUAGE** Find an underlined statement in the Photo Story with the same meaning as each of the following:

1 I'd prefer something cheaper. ....

2 This shop sells good things. ....

3 I don't know how to ask for a lower price. ....

4 I don't have much money. ....

5 Don't be afraid to bargain. ....

6 Here's a cheaper one. ....

SPEAKING

PAIR WORK Complete the chart with your opinions of the advantages and disadvantages of credit cards and cash. Then discuss your ideas with a partner.

An advantage of credit cards:	
A disadvantage of credit cards:	
An advantage of cash:	
A disadvantage of cash:	

GOAL Ask for a recommendation

GRAMMAR *Superlative adjectives*

Use superlative adjectives to compare more than two people, places, things, or ideas.

Which projector is **the cheapest** of these three? (**the** + an adjective + **est**)
Which brands are **the most** (or **least**) popular in your store? (**the most** / **least** + an adjective)

▶ 5:26 **Irregular forms**
good → better (than) → **the best**
bad → worse (than) → **the worst**

the most = ↑
the least = ↓

▶ 5:25

adjective	comparative	superlative	adjective	comparative	superlative
cheap	cheaper (than)	the cheapest	comfortable	more / less comfortable (than)	the most / least comfortable
nice	nicer (than)	the nicest	portable	more / less portable (than)	the most / least portable
easy	easier (than)	the easiest	difficult	more / less difficult (than)	the most / least difficult
big	bigger (than)	the biggest	expensive	more / less expensive (than)	the most / least expensive

GRAMMAR BOOSTER p. 140
• Comparatives and superlatives: usage and form

A **GRAMMAR PRACTICE** Read the salesperson's recommendations. Complete each statement, using the superlative form of the adjective.

1 The V5 is .... vacuum cleaner model from Zorax.
<u>new</u>

2 The Blendex is very inexpensive. It's .... blender we sell.
<u>cheap</u>

3 Compared to our other washing machines, the Laundrex 300 is ....
<u>easy to use</u>

4 The Focus C50 is .... digital camera we sell.
<u>popular</u>

5 The Vista PX is .... webcam you can buy.
<u>light</u>

6 Our customers say the My Juice 500 is .... juicer available today.
<u>practical</u>

7 You'll like the Morning Brew coffeemaker. It's .... to use.
<u>difficult</u>

8 If you don't want to spend a lot, the View Master is .... projector you can buy.
<u>expensive</u>

9 The Impress 400 isn't .... projector we have, but it <u>is</u> the best.
<u>expensive</u>

B **GRAMMAR PRACTICE** Complete the conversations. Use the superlative form of the adjectives.

1 A: All of these cameras are easy to use.
  B: But which is .... ?
  <u>small</u>

2 A: All of our ski sweaters are pretty warm.
  B: But I want a really heavy one. Which brand makes .... ones?
  <u>heavy</u>

3 A: She wrote at least six books about Italy.
  B: I know. But which of her books is .... ?
  <u>interesting</u>

4 A: Do you want to take a taxi, bus, or train to the airport?
  B: Which is .... ?
  <u>convenient</u>

5 A: You can study English at any school you want.
  B: OK. But which school is .... ?
  <u>good</u>

6 A: Here are three vacation packages you can choose from.
  B: That's nice. But just tell me which one is ....
  <u>affordable</u>

CONVERSATION MODEL

A ▶5:27 Read and listen to someone ask for a recommendation.

A: I'm looking for a pressure cooker. Which is the least expensive?

B: The Steam 2000. But it's not the best. How much do you want to spend?

A: No more than $100.

B: Well, we have some really good ones in your price range.

A: Great! Could I have a look?

B ▶5:28 **RHYTHM AND INTONATION** Listen again and repeat. Then practice the Conversation Model with a partner.

NOW YOU CAN Ask for a recommendation

DIGITAL VIDEO A **CONVERSATION ACTIVATOR** With a partner, change the Conversation Model. Use superlative adjectives. Use the ads, or your own real ads, to ask for a recommendation. Then change roles.

A: I'm looking for .... Which is the .... ?
B: The .... But it's not the .... How much do you want to spend?
A: No more than ....
B: Well, ...
A: ....

DON'T STOP!

Continue the conversation.
I'm also looking for [a coffeemaker].
Tell me about the [Brew King].
Do you accept credit cards?
Is there an ATM nearby?
I think I'll take the [Power X].

B **CHANGE PARTNERS** Ask for a recommendation for another type of product.

C **EXTENSION** Bring in newspaper ads for similar products. Use both comparative and superlative adjectives to discuss them.

Food Processors

Chop It 500
$120
Very popular!

Cooksmart $89
Easy to use

Whiz Kid
New! $200

Coffeemakers

Brew King $149
Very convenient!

Morningstar
$45
Small and practical

Cupster
$84
Popular

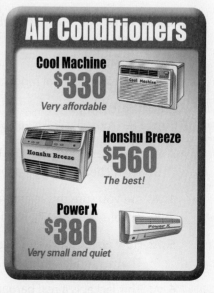

Air Conditioners

Cool Machine
$330
Very affordable

Honshu Breeze
$560
The best!

Power X
$380
Very small and quiet

GOAL Bargain for a lower price

CONVERSATION MODEL

A ▶5:29 Read and listen to someone bargain for a lower price.

A: How much do you want for that rug?

B: This one?

A: No. That one's not big enough. The other one.

B: 300.

A: That's a lot more than I want to spend. I can give you 200.

B: How about 225?

A: OK. That sounds fair.

B ▶5:30 **RHYTHM AND INTONATION** Listen again and repeat. Then practice the Conversation Model with a partner.

GRAMMAR *Too* and *enough*

When something is not satisfactory, use:

too + an adjective
Those rugs are **too small**.
That camera is **too heavy**.

OR

not + adjective + enough
Those rugs aren't **big enough**.
That camera isn't **light enough**.

When something is satisfactory, use an adjective + enough.
This coffeemaker is **small enough**. I'll take it.

> **Be careful!**
> Don't say: This coffeemaker is ~~enough small~~.

GRAMMAR BOOSTER p. 141
• Usage: <u>very</u>, <u>really</u>, and <u>too</u>

GRAMMAR PRACTICE Read the conversations between customers and salespeople. Then complete each conversation. Use <u>too</u> or <u>enough</u> and an adjective from the list.

1 A: My photocopier is .... I'm ready for an upgrade!
   B: OK. I have several models that are very fast. How much do you want to spend?

2 A: These jeans aren't .... They're very uncomfortable.
   B: I'm so sorry. Let me get you a larger size. Here you go.

3 A: I like these portable speakers, but they really aren't .... for travel.
   B: Then check out this pair. They're lighter, and you can have them for $20.

4 A: Are you sure this microwave is .... ? I'm a pretty busy guy.
   B: Absolutely. The X11 is our fastest model. And I can give you a great price.

5 A: How about this fan? Listen. It's very quiet.
   B: That's definitely .... for my bedroom. And it's very affordable. I'll take it.

6 A: This jacket is a real bargain, sir. It's only $692.
   B: $692? That's .... I don't want to spend that much.

Adjectives
big
cheap
expensive
fast
heavy
light
quiet
slow
small

PRONUNCIATION *Rising intonation for clarification*

A ▶5:31 Use rising intonation to ask for clarification. Read and listen. Then listen again and repeat.

1 A: Could I have a look at those bowls?

   B: These small ones?

   A: No, the big ones.

2 A: How much is that vase?

   B: This green one?

   A: That's right.

B PAIR WORK Place pairs of objects on your desk. Ask to have a look, and practice using rising intonation to ask for clarification.

66 Could I have a look at those sunglasses? 99

66 These brown ones? 99

VOCABULARY *How to bargain*

A ▶5:32 Read and listen. Then listen again and repeat.

Buyer's language	Seller's language
• How much do you want for that [shawl]? • That's more than I want to spend. • I can give you [twenty] for it. • Would you take [thirty]? • All I have is [forty]. • It's a deal.	• How much do you want to spend? • I could go as low as [seventy]. • I can't go lower than [sixty]. • You can have it for [fifty]. • How about [forty-five]? • It's a deal.

B ▶5:33 **LISTEN FOR DETAILS** Listen to people bargain. Complete each statement with the amount they agreed on and the type of item.

1 The buyer pays .... for the ....

2 The buyer pays .... for the ....

3 The buyer pays .... for the ....

4 The buyer pays .... for the ....

NOW YOU CAN Bargain for a lower price

A CONVERSATION ACTIVATOR With a partner, imagine that you are in a place where bargaining is common. One of you is the buyer, and the other is the seller. Use the Vocabulary and the photos, or your own ideas. Then change roles. Start like this:

A: How much do you want for .... ?

DON'T STOP!
• Ask about size, color, features, brand, etc.
• Use <u>too</u> and <u>enough</u>.
• Use superlatives.

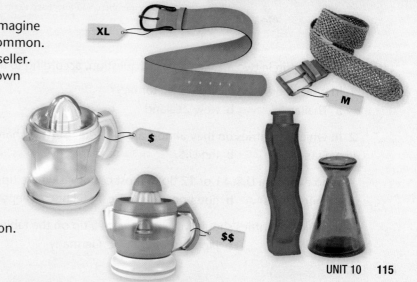

XL

M

$

$$

B CHANGE PARTNERS Create a new conversation. Bargain for the other items.

GOAL Discuss showing appreciation for service

BEFORE YOU READ

WARM-UP In your opinion, why is it important to understand the customs of other countries?

READING ▶ 5:34

When Should I Tip?

It's the question every traveler asks.

In some countries around the world, you never have to tip. But in most countries—at least 180 of them—tipping is customary, and the rules can be quite complicated.

Restaurants

In the U.S., restaurant servers expect a tip of 15 to 20% of the check—depending on how satisfied you are with the service. In most other countries, however, it's about 10%. In the U.S., you leave your tip on the table. But in Austria and Germany, it's considered rude if you don't hand the tip directly to the server.

In Europe, restaurants almost always add a service charge to the check, so you don't need to leave a separate tip. But in the U.S., a service charge is only added for groups of six or more people. So it's a good idea to look carefully at your check!

Taxis

In the U.S. and Canada, taxi drivers expect a tip of 15% of the taxi fare. However, in South America and many European countries, you don't usually tip taxi drivers. Instead, you can round off the fare and say, "Keep the change." (For example, if the fare is 3.80 euros, you just round it off to 4 euros.)

Hotels

What about the porter who carries your luggage? In Australia, you tip about AUS $3 (US $2) per bag. But in most countries, a tip of about US $1 is fine. You can also leave about US $1 to $2 a day for the housekeeper who cleans your hotel room.

So check the Internet for information on tipping customs before you travel. And remember: You *never* have to tip if the service is terrible.

FOR YOUR INFORMATION
Never tip in these countries:

Japan
Korea
Malaysia
New Zealand
Singapore
Thailand
United Arab Emirates
Vietnam

A CLASSIFY Circle <u>two</u> answers to each question, according to information in the Reading. Then explain.

1 In which countries is tipping customary?
   a Thailand   b New Zealand   c Australia   d Austria

2 In which countries do they almost always add a service charge to restaurant bills?
   a France   b the U.S.   c Germany   d United Arab Emirates

3 Who expects a U.S. $1 or $2 tip in most countries where tipping is customary?
   a hotel clerks   b hotel porters   c hotel housekeepers   d taxi drivers

4 In which countries should you never leave a tip on the table?
   a the U.S.   b Japan   c Germany   d Australia

B **DRAW CONCLUSIONS** Read each person's question. Give advice, according to the Reading. Underline the place in the Reading where you can find the information.

❝ My class is flying to a sports event in Canberra, Australia, next week. I have two large bags. **If a porter helps me, how much should I tip? ❞**

❝ I'm going to Chicago, in the U.S., on business. Let's say I take ten clients out for lunch and the bill is US $400. **How much more should I leave for the tip? ❞**

❝ I'm going to New Zealand. I'm staying in a nice hotel for about six days. **How much should I tip the housekeeper? ❞**

❝ I'm going to be in Toronto, Canada, this weekend. Someone told me the fare from the airport is CAN $43. **How much should I tip the driver? ❞**

DIGITAL
MORE
EXERCISES

C **APPLY INFORMATION** Imagine that you are visiting one of the countries in the Reading. Describe a situation in a restaurant, a taxi, or a hotel. Your classmates decide how much to tip.

NOW YOU CAN Discuss showing appreciation for service

A **FRAME YOUR IDEAS** How have you shown appreciation to someone for good service? Complete the questionnaire. Then tell a partner about your experiences.

- ☐ I left a tip.
- ☐ I gave a gift.
- ☐ I said "Thank you."
- ☐ I wrote a "thank-you" note.
- ☐ I sent an e-mail to the manager.
- ☐ Other: _____

❝ Last year, I went to a restaurant, and the waiter was really nice. At the end of the meal, I spoke to the manager about his great service. **❞**

B **NOTEPADDING** With a partner, write suggestions to a visitor to your country for how to show appreciation for good service. What should you do or say? Use your questionnaire above for examples.

Restaurant servers:	
Taxi drivers:	
Hotel housekeepers:	
Hotel luggage porters:	
Airport luggage porters:	
Other:	

C **DISCUSSION** Now discuss how to show appreciation for good service in your country. What are the customs? Does everyone agree?

Text-mining (optional)
Find and underline three words or phrases in the Reading that were new to you. Use them in your Discussion.
For example: "expect a tip."

GOAL Describe where to get the best deals

BEFORE YOU LISTEN

DIGITAL FLASH CARDS

A ▶5:35 **VOCABULARY** • *How to describe good and bad deals* Read and listen. Then listen again and repeat.

BZ-100
digital camera

Regular price: $179

Now on SALE for only

$169

$145.

$189.

Good deals

She **got a great deal**.

She **saved a lot of money**.

It **was a real bargain**.

Bad deals

He **got a bad deal**.

He **paid too much money**.

It **was a total rip-off**.

B **ACTIVATE NEW VOCABULARY** Read about two shopping experiences. With a partner, write a two-sentence summary of each story, using the Vocabulary.

On my last business trip, I wanted to buy a handmade rug. So I went to a store that had some really nice stuff. I found a beautiful one, but the asking price was too high: US $900. I'm not very good at bargaining, but I figured it couldn't hurt to ask. So I said, "I can go as high as $350." We bargained for a long time, but the merchant didn't come down in price. Finally, we shook hands, and I turned to leave the store. The merchant was very surprised, and he stopped me. I thought the handshake meant "Sorry. That's too low." But it really meant "It's a deal." So I bought it for $350.

When I was on vacation, I decided to look for an antique vase. I found a beautiful blue and white one from the sixteenth century. I bargained with the salesperson about the price, and she came way down for me. I was almost out of cash, but I bought it. It was a bit more than I wanted to spend, but I really liked it. Later, a friend told me that the "antiques" in these shops aren't really antiques—they're actually new! I guess I paid too much, but it's still a nice souvenir of my trip.

LISTENING COMPREHENSION

A ▶5:36 **LISTEN FOR MAIN IDEAS** Listen to the conversations about shopping. Then listen again and complete the chart.

	What did the shopper buy?	Did the shopper get a good price?	
1		☐ yes	☐ no
2		☐ yes	☐ no
3		☐ yes	☐ no
4		☐ yes	☐ no

B ▶5:37 **LISTEN FOR DETAILS** Listen again. Write the price each person paid.

1 .... euros   **2** .... pounds   **3** .... dollars   **4** .... pesos

A **NOTEPADDING** Complete the chart with notes about places in your city or town. Include an example or a reason for each opinion you write.

> **Where can you buy . . .**
> the most unusual gifts?
> The West Market has the coolest gifts! You can find anything there. And you can bargain for lower prices. I always love shopping there.

What are . . .	
the best restaurants?	the most expensive department stores?
the nicest hotels?	the most unusual markets?

Where can you buy . . .	
the best fruits and vegetables?	the least expensive clothes?
the coolest electronic products?	the most unusual gifts?

B **DISCUSSION** Compare your notes about places in your city or town and discuss where you can get the best deals.

> ❝ I think the fruits and vegetables at the North Market are the best in town. ❞

> ❝ Maybe. But you can save a lot of money at the South Market. They have the lowest prices there. ❞

A ▶5:38 Listen to each conversation. Write the item that the people are talking about. Indicate whether the item is satisfactory (✓) or not satisfactory (✗) to the customer. Then listen again and circle the adjectives that the salesperson uses to describe the product.

	They're talking about . . .	Satisfactory?	Adjectives
1		☐	light / fast / cheap
2		☐	light / warm / beautiful
3		☐	tall / beautiful / affordable
4		☐	light / easy to use / affordable

B Complete the sentences.

1 If you're out of cash and the bank is closed, you can get money from ....

2 If there's a service charge on your check, you probably don't need to leave ....

3 In some places, you can .... for a lower price.

4 Before you travel to a foreign country, you should check the .... of your currency and the currency of the place you're traveling to.

5 I got a real .... I saved a lot of money.

6 It was a total .... I paid too much money.

C Rewrite each sentence, using <u>too</u> or <u>enough</u>. For example:

That vase is too heavy.

> *That vase isn't light enough.*

1 Those cameras aren't cheap enough.

2 This printer is too slow.

3 The inside of the fridge isn't cool enough.

4 That restaurant is too noisy.

5 My flat screen TV isn't big enough.

6 Those pants aren't long enough.

D Write two sentences about shopping in your city or town. Use the superlative.

> 1 | *The stores in Old Town have the most interesting gifts.*

1	
2	

WRITING

Write a guide to the best places for a visitor to your city or town to stay in, visit, and shop.

Ideas
hotels   theaters
stores   neighborhoods
museums   stadiums

WRITING BOOSTER   p. 148
• Connecting contradictory ideas
• Guidance for this writing exercise

For additional language practice . . .

♫ TOP NOTCH POP   • Lyrics p. 150
"Shopping for Souvenirs"

DIGITAL SONG   DIGITAL KARAOKE

Al's Electronics

SALE!

CoolRay 6
Super thin
US $350

Now US $220

Easy to use
Only 3 oz / .085 kg

Basik XT
So Fast!
US $980

Now US $950

Very Professional
Only 24 oz / .68 kg

EasyPix 500
Very Popular
US $220

Now US $180

Only 4.1 oz / .12 kg

SALE!

Dazio 420
Brightness: 2000 lumens
Very portable
US $1,199

Now US $999

Only 2.8 lb / 1.27 kg

Clearview 3Z
Brightness: 2000 lumens
Really affordable
US $899

Now US $849

Only 4 lb / 1.81 kg

Manna T-20
Brightness: 4000 lumens
So powerful!
US $3,999

Now US $3,899

Only 3.5 lb / 1.59 kg

SALE!

Cloud 9
50" / 127 cm
Like it loud? This is the one!
US $1,399

Now US $1,149

Runex
19" / 48 cm
Very portable
US $399

Now US $229

Washburn
32" / 81 cm
Brand new!
US $699

Now US $599

ORAL REVIEW

CONTEST Form teams. Create false statements about the products. Another team corrects the statements. (One point for each correction.) For example:

A: The EasyPix 500 is the lightest camera.
B: No. The CoolRay 6 is the lightest one.

ROLE PLAY Create conversations for the people.

- Ask for a recommendation. Start like this:
  I'm looking for ___. Which is the . . . ?
- Bargain for the best price. Start like this:
  How much do you want for that . . . ?

GIFTS 'N THINGS

✓ NOW I CAN

- ☐ Ask for a recommendation.
- ☐ Bargain for a lower price.
- ☐ Discuss showing appreciation for service.
- ☐ Describe where to get the best deals.

Reference Charts

COUNTRIES AND NATIONALITIES

Country	Nationality	Country	Nationality	Country	Nationality
Argentina	Argentinean / Argentine	Guatemala	Guatemalan	Peru	Peruvian
Australia	Australian	Holland	Dutch	Poland	Polish
Belgium	Belgian	Honduras	Honduran	Portugal	Portuguese
Bolivia	Bolivian	Hungary	Hungarian	Russia	Russian
Brazil	Brazilian	India	Indian	Saudi Arabia	Saudi / Saudi Arabian
Canada	Canadian	Indonesia	Indonesian	Spain	Spanish
Chile	Chilean	Ireland	Irish	Sweden	Swedish
China	Chinese	Italy	Italian	Switzerland	Swiss
Colombia	Colombian	Japan	Japanese	Taiwan	Chinese
Costa Rica	Costa Rican	Korea	Korean	Thailand	Thai
Ecuador	Ecuadorian	Lebanon	Lebanese	Turkey	Turkish
Egypt	Egyptian	Malaysia	Malaysian	the United Kingdom	British
El Salvador	Salvadorean	Mexico	Mexican	the United States	American
France	French	Nicaragua	Nicaraguan	Uruguay	Uruguayan
Germany	German	Panama	Panamanian	Venezuela	Venezuelan
Greece	Greek	Paraguay	Paraguayan	Vietnam	Vietnamese

NON-COUNT NOUNS

This list is an at-a-glance reference to the non-count nouns used in *Top Notch 1*.

aerobics
air conditioning
basketball
beef
bike riding
bread
broccoli
butter
cake
candy
cash

cheese
chicken
clothing
coffee
crab
culture
dancing
dessert
dinner
electronics
English

entertainment
fish
food
fruit
garlic
golf
health
history
hosiery
hot sauce
housework

ice
ice cream
juice
junk food
lamb
lettuce
lingerie
meat
milk
music
nature

oil
outerwear
pasta
pepper
pie
rice
running
salad
salt
sausage
seafood

service
shopping
shrimp
sightseeing
skydiving
sleepwear
soccer
soup
squid
swimming
tennis

traffic
transportation
TV
walking
water
weather
wildlife
yogurt

IRREGULAR VERBS

base form	simple past	past participle	base form	simple past	past participle	base form	simple past	past participle
be	was / were	been	give	gave	given	sell	sold	sold
begin	began	begun	go	went	gone	send	sent	sent
break	broke	broken	grow	grew	grown	shake	shook	shaken
bring	brought	brought	have	had	had	sing	sang	sung
build	built	built	hear	heard	heard	sit	sat	sat
buy	bought	bought	hit	hit	hit	sleep	slept	slept
catch	caught	caught	hurt	hurt	hurt	speak	spoke	spoken
choose	chose	chosen	keep	kept	kept	spend	spent	spent
come	came	come	know	knew	known	stand	stood	stood
cost	cost	cost	leave	left	left	steal	stole	stolen
cut	cut	cut	lose	lost	lost	swim	swam	swum
do	did	done	make	made	made	take	took	taken
drink	drank	drunk	mean	meant	meant	teach	taught	taught
drive	drove	driven	meet	met	met	tell	told	told
eat	ate	eaten	pay	paid	paid	think	thought	thought
fall	fell	fallen	put	put	put	throw	threw	thrown
feel	felt	felt	quit	quit	quit	understand	understood	understood
find	found	found	read	read	read	wake up	woke up	woken up
fit	fit	fit	ride	rode	ridden	wear	wore	worn
fly	flew	flown	run	ran	run	win	won	won
forget	forgot	forgotten	say	said	said	write	wrote	written
get	got	gotten	see	saw	seen			

Grammar Booster

The Grammar Booster is optional. It offers a variety of information and extra practice. Sometimes it further explains or expands the Unit grammar and points out common errors. In other cases, it reviews and practices previously learned grammar that would be helpful when learning new grammar concepts. If you use the Grammar Booster, you will find extra exercises in the Workbook in a separate section labeled Grammar Booster. The Grammar Booster content is not tested on any *Top Notch* tests.

 **UNIT 1** *Lesson 1*

Information questions with <u>be</u>: usage and form

Use <u>Who</u> to ask about people, <u>What</u> to ask about things, <u>Where</u> to ask about places, and <u>How old</u> to ask about age.

Singular nouns	Plural nouns
Who's your teacher?	Who **are** the new students?
What's your name?	What **are** their names?
Where's your father from?	Where **are** your classmates from?
How old **is** your sister?	How old **are** your children?

A Choose an answer for each question.

_____ 1 What's your name?   a Scotland, actually. She's British.

_____ 2 Where is she from?   b He's the CEO of BRC Incorporated.

_____ 3 Where's her father from?   c Kim's father? Seoul, I think.

_____ 4 Who is Bernard Udall?   d Eighteen and ten.

_____ 5 How old are your cousins?   e Ivan. But everyone calls me Vanya.

Possessive nouns and adjectives

Possessive nouns

Add <u>'s</u> to a name or a noun.
     Where is **Peter's** father from?   What's the **teacher's** name?

Add an apostrophe (') to plural nouns that end in <u>-s</u>.
     What are the **students'** names?

Add <u>'s</u> to the name or noun that comes last in a list of two or more.
     When is **Sally and Hannah's** class?

I	→	my
you	→	your
he	→	his
she	→	her
it	→	its
we	→	our
they	→	their

Possessive adjectives
     Where's Chad's father from? → Where's **his** father from?
     What's Sheila's last name? → What's **her** last name?
     What's Lee and Ping's address? → What's **their** address?

B Complete each sentence with a possessive form of the noun.

1 .... (Dean) father is an engineer.

2 What is .... (Janec) e-mail address?

3 The book is .... (Kayla).

4 .... (Nicole and Sean) class is at eight.

5 What are your .... (brothers) occupations?

C On a separate sheet of paper, write a question for each answer, using <u>What</u> and a possessive adjective.

1 My occupation? I'm a student.   *What's your occupation?*

2 Lin and Ben's? It's 2 Bay Street.   5 Sandra's nickname? It's Sandy.

3 His phone number? It's 21-66-55.   6 My e-mail address? It's acme4@ymail.com.

4 Dave's last name? It's Bourne.   7 Ray's? His address is 456 Rue Noire.

D Complete each sentence with a possessive adjective.

1 This is my sister. .... husband is from Ecuador.

2 Robert is a new student here. .... nickname is Bobby.

3 My friends live in London, but .... hometown is in Scotland.

4 My husband and I live in Chicago, but .... children don't.

5 I'd like you to meet .... colleague Sam. He works with me at the bank.

6 I like that picture. .... colors are very nice.

UNIT 1 *Lesson 2*

Verb *be*: usage and form

The verb *be* gives information about the subject of a sentence. The subject of a sentence can be a noun or a pronoun.

noun subject	pronoun subject
Our teacher is from the United States.	**She** is from the United States.
That school is new.	**It** is new.

Affirmative statements
There are three forms of the verb *be* in the present tense: *am*, *is*, and *are*.

I am a student.	He She is late. It	You We are married. They

Contracted forms
Contract *be* with subject nouns and pronouns. Use contractions in speaking and informal writing.

Robin is an artist. = **Robin's** an artist.
He is single. = **He's** single.

I am a student. = **I'm** a student.
You are on time. = **You're** on time.

Negative contractions
There are two ways to form negative contractions.

He's **not** Brazilian. = He **isn't** Brazilian.
They're **not** teachers. = They **aren't** teachers.

Note: There is only one way to contract I am not → I'm not.

Short answers with *be*: common errors

Don't use contractions with affirmative short answers to *yes* / *no* questions.

Are you a salesperson?	Yes, I am. NOT ~~Yes, I'm.~~
Is he American?	Yes, he is. NOT ~~Yes, he's.~~
Are they designers?	Yes, they are. NOT ~~Yes, they're.~~

Note: It is also common to answer just with **Yes** or **No**.
Are you a salesperson?   Yes.

A On a separate sheet of paper, rewrite the sentences, using contractions. Then practice saying each sentence aloud.

1 She is an opera singer.
2 They are managers.

3 I am a student.
4 Bart is from Australia.

5 My mother is late.
6 Your father is nice.

B On a separate sheet of paper, write a short answer for each question.

1 Is New York in Russia?
2 Are you a scientist?
3 Are Korea and Japan in Asia?

4 Is Italy a city?
5 Is it 3:00 right now?
6 Are you a student?

7 Are you Canadian?
8 Is your father a manager?
9 Is English difficult?

Prepositions of time and place: usage rules

Time

Use on with the names of days or dates.

on Thursday	on Monday morning	on New Year's Day	on May 3rd
on the weekend	on Sundays	on a weekday	

Use in with periods of time (but not with names of days).

in 2008	in July	in [the] spring	in an hour
in the morning	in the 20th century	in the 1950s	in two weeks

Use at with specific moments in time.

at 9:00	at dawn	at noon
at sunrise	at dusk	at midnight

Place

Use on with the names of streets and specific physical locations.

on Main Street	on Smith Avenue	on the corner
on the street	on the right	on the left

Use in with the names of cities, countries, continents, and other large locations.

in the neighborhood	in the center of town	in Lima	in front of the school
in Korea	in Africa	in the ocean	

Use at for buildings and addresses.

at the theater	at the supermarket	at the bank
at the train station	at 10 Main Street	

Use at for general locations of activity.

at home	at work	at school

A Complete the sentences with <u>on</u>, <u>in</u>, or <u>at</u>.

1 A: When's the movie?
 B: The movie is .... Friday .... 8:30.

2 A: Where is he?
 B: He's not here right now. He's .... work.

3 A: Where's his office?
 B: It's .... the center of town.

4 A: When was her mother born?
 B: She was born .... January 1.

5 A: When does the movie take place?
 B: It takes place .... the 19th century .... Africa.

6 .... the weekend, I'm going to the concert .... the public library.

7 The park opens .... 6:00 .... the morning and closes .... dusk.

8 Is the concert hall .... Grove Street?

9 I think the theater is .... the right side of the street.

10 Let's go to the evening show. The concert is outside, and the weather is really hot .... the afternoon.

11 This concert occurs every second year .... November.

12 I'll see you .... Thursday morning in front of the theater, OK?

B Look at the tickets. On a separate sheet of paper, write questions with <u>When</u> or <u>What time</u>. Write a question with <u>Where</u>.

You can express a preference for an activity with <u>would like to</u> + a verb.

Statements
> I'd like to go to the movies tonight.
> She'd like to see a play.
> They wouldn't like to be late.

Questions and answers

Would you like to go to the lecture with me?	Yes, I would. / No, I wouldn't.
Would your parents like to see this movie?	Yes, they would. / No, they wouldn't.
What would you like to download?	Some good Peruvian folk music.
Where would he like to go?	To the concert in the park.
When would they like to leave?	At about 9:00 in the morning.
Who would you like to invite to the rock concert?	All my friends.
BUT Who would like to go to a play tonight?	We would!

Remember: You can also use <u>would like</u> + a noun to state a preference:
> I'd like coffee. / Would you like tea?

Contractions
> I would like ➔ I'd like
> We would not like ➔ We wouldn't like

Be careful! Don't contract <u>would</u> in affirmative short answers.
> Would you like to listen to music? Yes, I would. NOT Yes, I̶'̶d̶.

C Complete the conversations with <u>would like to</u> + a verb. Use contractions when possible.

1 A: .... (see) *Frozen* this evening?

B: Sorry. No, I .... I'm not an animated movie fan.

2 A: .... (go) to the concert with us?

B: Yes, they ....

3 A: Who .... (eat) dinner at Mario's Restaurant?

B: We .... !

4 A: .... you .... (download) a music video?

B: Sounds good! Yes, I ....

5 A: What .... your sister .... (do) this afternoon after class?

B: She .... (hang out) with her friends for an hour before dinner.

6 A: When .... your teacher .... (show) the video?

B: He .... (show) the video tomorrow morning in class.

UNIT 3 *Lesson 1*

Usage
Use the simple present tense to talk about facts and habitual actions in the present.

facts	habitual actions
Josh speaks Spanish very well.	Josh speaks Spanish every day.
They work at Coffee Central.	They work late on Fridays.

Form
Add <u>-s</u> to the base form of the verb for third-person singular (<u>he</u>, <u>she</u>, or <u>it</u>).

I like Thai food.	He likes Peruvian food.
You study English.	She studies French.
They open at 6:00.	The store opens at 8:00.
We work at a café.	Marlene works at a school.

A Write negative statements.

1 Gwen likes classical music. (her sister) *Her sister doesn't like classical music.*

2 The café closes at 6:00. (the bookstore) ....

3 Neal lives in Quito. (his sister) ....

4 Miles works in an office. (his brother) ....

5 I have a big family. (my husband) ....

6 My younger brother speaks Chinese. (I) ....

7 Kiko's nephew likes hip-hop. (her niece) ....

B Write <u>yes</u> / <u>no</u> questions.

1 **A:** *Does your sister live* .... near you?

   B: No, she doesn't. She lives in another city.

2 **A:** .... drink coffee?

   B: No, he doesn't. My brother drinks tea.

3 **A:** .... children?

   B: No. We don't have any yet.

4 **A:** .... in Mexico?

   B: No. My in-laws live in Chile.

5 **A:** .... English?

   B: Yes, she does. My niece speaks it well.

6 **A:** .... work here?

   B: Yes, they do. My cousins work downstairs.

7 **A:** .... early?

   B: No. The bookstore opens late.

UNIT 3 *Lesson 2*

Information questions in the simple present tense: form and common errors

<u>Do</u> and <u>does</u>

Use <u>do</u> or <u>does</u> + the base form of a verb to ask information questions.

Where **do** your in-laws **live**?   Where **does** your sister-in-law **live**?

When **do** you **visit** your cousins?   When **does** she **visit** her nieces?

How often **do** they **go** to class?   How often **does** he **go** to class?

Questions with <u>Who</u>

Compare these questions with <u>Who</u>.

Who visits your aunt in Chicago?   **My mother** does. (My mother = subject)

Who does your mother visit in Chicago?   My mother visits **my aunt**. (my aunt = object)

Be careful! Don't use <u>do</u> or <u>does</u> with <u>Who</u> if the question is about the subject. Always use the third-person singular form to ask questions with <u>Who</u> about the subject.

Who lives here? NOT Who ~~does live~~ here? NOT Who ~~live~~ here?

<u>How many</u>

Be careful! Always use <u>How many</u> with plural nouns.

How many cousins do you have? NOT How many ~~cousin~~ do you have?

Complete the information questions.

1 A: .... your uncle .... ?
   B: He's a doctor.

2 A: .... your in-laws .... ?
   B: They live in Seoul.

3 A: .... cousins .... ?
   B: I have ten of them.

4 A: .... your parents?
   B: I visit them every weekend.

5 A: .... your stepsister .... ?
   B: She lives across the street.

6 A: .... speaks Russian?
   B: My brother-in-law does.

7 A: .... your niece .... with?
   B: She lives with my aunt.

8 A: .... you .... ?
   B: I study late at night.

9 A: .... has three kids?
   B: My younger sister does.

10 A: .... your older brother .... ?
    B: He studies in London.

UNIT 4 Lesson 1

Non-count nouns: expressing quantities

We can make many non-count nouns countable:
   a slice of bread, a loaf of bread, three pieces of bread, two kinds of bread

The following phrases are used with non-count nouns in order to make them countable:
   liquids: a glass of, two cups of, a liter of, six gallons of, a bottle of, a can of
   solids: a cup of, a piece of, three slices of, a kilo of, a spoonful of

A   Complete each statement with a countable quantity. (Note: More than one phrase of quantity may be possible.)

liquids

1 This soup is so creamy. It has two ....
   milk in it.

2 She must be very thirsty. This is her third
   .... water.

3 My car has a big gas tank. It holds .... gas.

solids

4 I ate .... cheese, and now I feel sick.

5 A club sandwich doesn't have two .... bread.
   It has three .... bread.

6 I like my tea sweet. Please put in .... sugar.

Some and any

Use some and any to describe an indefinite number or amount.
   There are some apples in the fridge. (Indefinite number: we don't know how many.)
   Are there any oranges? (Indefinite number: no specific number being asked about.)
   They are bringing us some coffee. (Indefinite amount: we don't know how much.)

Use some with non-count nouns and with plural count nouns in affirmative statements.
          non-count noun plural count noun
   We need some milk and some bananas.

Use any with non-count nouns and plural count nouns in negative statements.
          non-count noun   plural count noun
   We don't want any cheese, and we don't need any apples.

Use any or some in questions with count and non-count nouns. There is no difference in meaning.
   Do you need any cookies or butter?   Do you need some cookies or butter?

B   Change the sentences from affirmative to negative.

1 There is some coffee in the kitchen. *There isn't any coffee in the kitchen.* ....

2 There are some onions on the table. ....

3 We have some cookies. ....

4 They need some onions for the soup. ....

5 She's buying some fruit at the market. ....

6 The Reeds want some eggs for breakfast. ....

7 I want some butter on my sandwich. ....

8 There is some chicken in the fridge. ....

9 They need some cheese for the pasta. ....

C Complete each sentence with <u>some</u> or <u>any</u>.

1 I don't want .... more coffee, thank you.

2 There isn't .... salt in this soup.

3 We don't see .... sandwiches on the menu.

4 They need .... sugar for their tea.

5 The restaurant is making .... pies for the party.

6 It's too bad that there isn't .... soup.

7 I don't see .... menus on those tables.

8 There are .... eggs for the omelette.

Questions with *How much* and *How many*

Ask questions with <u>How much</u> for non-count nouns. Ask questions with <u>How many</u> for count nouns.

How much rice is in the soup?	Not much. Two cups.
How many eggs are in the fridge?	Not many. Three.

D Complete each question with <u>How much</u> or <u>How many</u>.

1 .... bread do we need?

2 .... salt did you put in the beef stew?

3 .... hot pepper do you like?

4 .... spoonfuls of sugar do you want in your tea?

5 .... oil should I put in this salad?

6 .... cheese is there in the fridge?

7 .... slices of bread do you want?

8 .... cups of coffee did you drink?

Words that can be count nouns or non-count nouns

Some nouns can be used as count or non-count nouns. The word is the same, but the meaning is different.

non-count use	count use
Chicken is delicious.	I bought two **chickens**.
Let's watch **TV**.	We have three **TVs** in our house.
The sun provides **light**.	It's too bright in here. Turn off one of the **lights**.

Some words can have a count sense or a non-count sense with only a slight difference in meaning.

I'm in the mood for **salad**.   OR   I'm in the mood for **a salad**.

I'd like **steak** for dinner.   OR   I'd like **a steak** for dinner.

Plural count nouns: spelling rules

Add -s to most nouns.

cup   **cups**   appetizer   **appetizers**   apple   **apples**

If a noun ends in a consonant and -y, change the y to i and add -es.

cherry   **cherries**   berry   **berries**

BUT: Do not change the y when the letter before the y is a vowel.

boy   **boys**

Add -es to nouns that end in -ch, -o, -s, -sh, or -x.

lunch	**lunches**	radish	**radishes**	tomato	**tomatoes**
box	**boxes**	glass	**glasses**		

E Write the plural form of each count noun.

1 clam ....

2 snack ....

3 cup ....

4 olive ....

5 spoonful ....

6 pear ....

7 french fry ....

8 sandwich ....

9 vegetable ....

10 potato ....

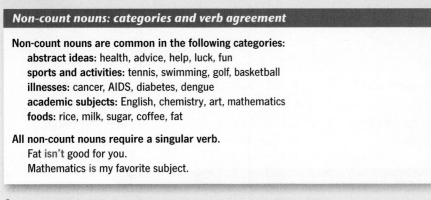

Non-count nouns: categories and verb agreement

Non-count nouns are common in the following categories:
   abstract ideas: health, advice, help, luck, fun
   sports and activities: tennis, swimming, golf, basketball
   illnesses: cancer, AIDS, diabetes, dengue
   academic subjects: English, chemistry, art, mathematics
   foods: rice, milk, sugar, coffee, fat

All non-count nouns require a singular verb.
   Fat **isn't** good for you.
   Mathematics **is** my favorite subject.

A Complete each sentence with the correct form of the verb.

1 Coffee .... (be) my favorite beverage.

2 Rice .... (be) very good for you, even when you are sick.

3 Mathematics .... (create) problems for many students, but not for me!

4 Influenza .... (cause) pain and fever.

5 Darkness .... (frighten) some people, but I don't know why.

6 Medical advice .... (help) people decide what to do about their health.

B Complete the sentences with <u>a</u> or <u>an</u>. If the noun is a non-count noun, write an **✗**.

1 He has .... diabetes.

2 She would like to eat .... banana.

3 "................ apple a day keeps the doctor away."

4 Would you like .... appetizer?

5 There's .... egg on the shelf.

6 Does the restaurant serve .... rice with the chicken?

7 He always gives .... good advice.

8 My family loves .... music.

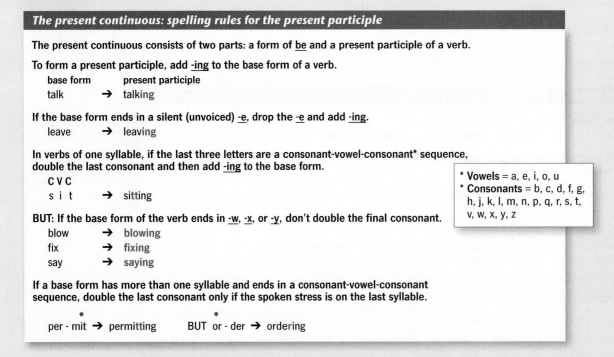

The present continuous: spelling rules for the present participle

The present continuous consists of two parts: a form of <u>be</u> and a present participle of a verb.

To form a present participle, add <u>-ing</u> to the base form of a verb.
   base form   present participle
   talk   ➔   talking

If the base form ends in a silent (unvoiced) <u>-e</u>, drop the <u>-e</u> and add <u>-ing</u>.
   leave   ➔   leaving

In verbs of one syllable, if the last three letters are a consonant-vowel-consonant* sequence, double the last consonant and then add <u>-ing</u> to the base form.
   C V C
   s i t   ➔   sitting

   * **Vowels** = a, e, i, o, u
   * **Consonants** = b, c, d, f, g, h, j, k, l, m, n, p, q, r, s, t, v, w, x, y, z

BUT: If the base form of the verb ends in <u>-w</u>, <u>-x</u>, or <u>-y</u>, don't double the final consonant.
   blow   ➔   blowing
   fix   ➔   fixing
   say   ➔   saying

If a base form has more than one syllable and ends in a consonant-vowel-consonant sequence, double the last consonant only if the spoken stress is on the last syllable.

   per - mit ➔ permitting   BUT or - der ➔ ordering

A Write the present participle for each base form. Follow the rules.

1 turn	**7** stop	**13** sew	**19** change ....
2 rain	**8** exit	**14** listen	**20** be ....
3 run	**9** sit	**15** do	**21** have ....
4 help	**10** eat	**16** write	**22** put ....
5 open	**11** buy	**17** begin	**23** go ....
6 close	**12** mix	**18** use	**24** pay ....

The present continuous: rules for forming statements

Remember to form the present continuous with <u>be</u> and a present participle of a verb.

Affirmative statements	**Negative statements**
I'm studying English.	I'm not studying French.
You're studying French.	You're not studying English.
He's reading a book.	He's not reading a newspaper.
She's reading a newspaper.	She's not reading a book.
We're watching TV.	We're not watching a DVD.
They're watching a video.	They're not watching TV.

B On a separate sheet of paper, change each affirmative statement to a negative statement. Use contractions.

1 She's going to the supermarket.

2 He's calling his wife this afternoon.

3 I'm cooking dinner tonight.

4 The Roberts are feeding their kids early.

5 Joel's taking the bus to the movies.

6 We're getting a new printer.

C Write answers to the questions in complete affirmative or negative statements. Use the present continuous and contractions.

1 Are you studying English this weekend? ....

2 When are you taking a vacation? ....

3 Is it raining now? ....

4 Where are you eating dinner tonight? ....

5 Are you listening to music now? ....

6 Who's making breakfast tomorrow? ....

The present continuous: rules for forming questions

<u>Yes</u> / <u>no</u> questions: Place a form of <u>be</u> before the subject of the sentence.

Is she watching TV?	Are we meeting this afternoon?
Are you driving there?	Are they talking on the phone?
Is Stu shopping?	Are Nan and Bert studying?

Information questions: Use question words to ask information questions.

When are you going?	How much are you paying for that computer?
What are you doing right now?	Why are you buying that laptop?
Who is he watching on TV?	

Be careful! The word order changes when using <u>Who</u> to ask a question about the subject:
Who's talking on the phone? (John is.)

D Write a question in the present continuous to complete each conversation.

1 A: .... ?
   B: No. Luke's not watching TV right now.

2 A: .... ?
   B: Yes. She's working this morning.

3 A: .... ?
   B: I'm calling Janet Hammond.

4 A: .... ?
   B: She's coming home later tonight.

Can and Have to: form and common errors

Be careful!

It **has to** close at 4:00.
NOT ~~It has to closes.~~
NOT ~~It has to closing.~~

Does he **have to** go?
NOT ~~Does he have to goes?~~
NOT ~~Does he has to go?~~

Be careful! Use can with the base form of a verb.

She **can play** golf very well.
NOT ~~She can plays.~~
NOT ~~She can to play.~~

Can he **play** tennis?
NOT ~~Can he plays?~~
NOT ~~Can he to play?~~

There are three negative forms of can.

He **can't** swim. = He **cannot** swim. = He **can not** swim.

Remember:

I You They We	have to go to class at 9:00.
She He	has to go to class at 8:00.

A Correct the sentences.

come
1 Can they ~~coming~~ to the movie next week?

2 My mother-in-law have to go shopping this afternoon.

3 My cousin can't plays soccer tomorrow.

4 Does he has to meet his niece at the airport?

5 We're going to the beach this weekend, but I no can swim.

6 Alex can to go out for dinner tonight.

7 She doesn't have to working late tomorrow.

She cans go out for dinner.

8 Can he visits his in-laws next weekend?

9 You have to filling out an application for your

English class.

10 Do we have to studying now? We're watching TV.

Can and have to: information questions

Can

Where **can** I **play** soccer around here? (Try the park.)
When **can** they **come** for lunch? (After class.)
How often **can** we **go** running? (Any time. Our afternoons are free.)
What languages **can** she **speak**? (She can speak Italian and Russian.)

Have to

What **does** he **have to do** tomorrow? (He has to go shopping.)
How often **does** she **have to work** late? (Not often.)
When **do** they **have to buy** the tickets? (This afternoon.)
Where **do** you **have to go** this morning? (To the airport.)

Be careful! See the difference when Who is the object or the subject.

Who **can** John **visit** on the weekend? He can visit **his cousins**. (object)
Who **can visit** his cousins on the weekend? **John** can. (subject)
Who **do** you **have to call**? I have to call **my boss**. (object)
Who **has to write** the report? **My boss** does. (subject)

B Complete the questions, using the cues and <u>can</u>.

1 A: .... basketball?
   (where / I / play)
   B: Try the school. It isn't far.

2 A: .... dinner?
   (when / we / have)
   B: How about tomorrow night?

3 A: .... walking?
   (where / I / go)
   B: You can go to the park. It's very nice.

4 A: .... ?
   (how often / you / exercise)
   B: Not as much as I'd like to. I'm too busy.

5 A: .... breakfast?
   (who / make)
   B: What about Bill? He wakes up early.

6 A: .... with about classes?
   (who / I / speak)
   B: The receptionist can help you.

C Complete the questions and answers, using a form of <u>have to</u>.

1 A: .... he .... (do) tomorrow?

  B: He .... (go) to class.

2 A: .... she .... (call) the office?

  B: She .... (call) every morning.

3 A: .... he .... (go) to the airport?

  B: He .... (leave) here at 3:00.

4 A: .... they .... (send) the form to?

  B: They can't send it. They .... (take) it to the office.

5 A: .... you .... (meet) after class?

  B: I .... (meet) my sister. We're going to the movies.

6 A: .... (help) the teacher after class?

  B: Chris and Tania. They .... (clean) the board.

<u>Can and be able to</u>: present and past forms

You can also use <u>be able to</u> + base form for ability or possibility. <u>Can</u> is more frequent in spoken language.

I **can play** the violin. = I'm **able to play** the violin. (ability)

Bill **can meet** you at six. = Bill **is able to meet** you at six. (possibility)

He **can't swim**. = He **isn't able to swim**. (ability)

They **can't call** this afternoon. = They **aren't able to call** this afternoon. (possibility)

Use <u>could</u> or <u>was / were able to</u> + base form to talk about the past.

When I was four I **could ride** a bike (or **was able to ride** a bike).

They **could speak** (or **were able to speak**) French before they were ten.

She **couldn't be** (or **wasn't able to be**) there yesterday because she had a meeting.

We **couldn't understand** (or **weren't able to understand**) the directions.

Be careful! Use <u>was / were able to</u> (**NOT** <u>could</u>) for affirmative past statements of *possibility*.

She **was able to be** there yesterday. NOT She ~~could be~~ there yesterday.

D On a separate sheet of paper, change <u>can</u> to <u>be able to</u> in the sentences.

1 She can swim very well.

2 They can't ride a bicycle.

3 I can't finish this report today.

4 George can meet you at the airport.

5 Lucy can't take the bus to the mall.

6 We can call you before the meeting.

E On a separate sheet of paper, change the statements from the present to the past. More than one correct answer may be possible.

1 We're able to help him.

2 The Martins can't go to the concert.

3 She is able to be there at seven.

4 Nicole can cook for the party.

5 Rachel and Brooke aren't able to play basketball at the school.

UNIT 6 *Lesson 2*

The simple present tense: non-action verbs

Some verbs are non-action verbs. Most non-action verbs are not usually used in the present continuous, even when they are describing something that is happening right now.

I **want** a sandwich. NOT I ~~am wanting~~ a sandwich.

Some non-action verbs have action and non-action meanings.

non-action meaning	action meaning
I **have** two sandwiches. (possession)	I'm **having** a sandwich. (eating)
I **think** English is easy. (opinion)	I'm **thinking** about her. (the act of thinking)

Some non-action verbs

be	miss
have	need
know	see
like	understand
love	want

A Complete the message. Use the simple present tense or the present continuous form of the verbs.

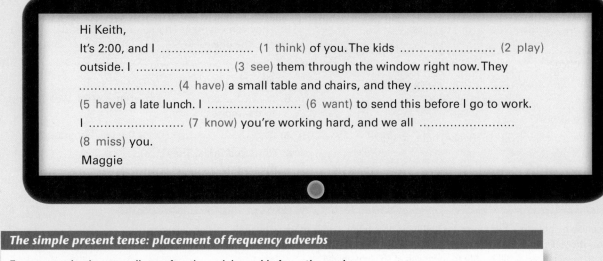

Hi Keith,

It's 2:00, and I .... (1 think) of you. The kids .... (2 play) outside. I .... (3 see) them through the window right now. They .... (4 have) a small table and chairs, and they .... (5 have) a late lunch. I .... (6 want) to send this before I go to work. I .... (7 know) you're working hard, and we all .... (8 miss) you.

Maggie

The simple present tense: placement of frequency adverbs

Frequency adverbs generally go after the verb <u>be</u> and before other verbs.
I **am usually** at the pool on Saturdays.
I **usually go** to the pool on Saturdays.

<u>Sometimes</u>, <u>usually</u>, <u>often</u>, <u>generally</u>, and <u>occasionally</u> can also go at the beginning or end of a sentence.
Sometimes I go to the mall on Saturdays.
I go to the pool **occasionally**.

Be careful! Don't use <u>never</u> or <u>always</u> at the beginning or end of a sentence.
Don't say: ~~Never I go to the pool.~~ OR ~~I go to the pool always.~~

In negative sentences, most frequency adverbs can go before or after <u>don't</u> or <u>doesn't</u>.
Hank **usually doesn't** go running on the weekend.
Hank **doesn't usually** go running on the weekend.

Be careful! The frequency adverb <u>always</u> cannot go before <u>don't</u> or <u>doesn't</u>.
I **don't always** have breakfast in the morning. NOT I ~~always don't~~ have breakfast in the morning.

Be careful! Use the frequency adverb <u>never</u> or <u>not</u> + <u>ever</u> to form the negative. Don't use <u>never</u> with a negative verb.
I **never eat** sweets. OR I **don't ever** eat sweets. NOT I ~~don't never eat~~ sweets.

Time expressions

Time expressions generally go at the beginning or end of a sentence. When a time expression is at the beginning, a comma is optional. Don't use a comma when the time expression is at the end.
Three times a week, I go to the pool.   I go to the pool **three times a week**.

The time expression <u>a lot</u> goes at the end of a sentence.
I go to the pool **a lot**. NOT ~~A lot I go to the pool~~.

Some time expressions
every week
every other day
once a month
twice a year
three times a week

Other expressions
once in a while
a lot

B On a separate sheet of paper, rewrite the sentences correctly.

1 She plays usually golf on Sunday.
2 They go to the park hardly ever.
3 I always am hungry in the afternoon.
4 We once in a while have eggs for breakfast.
5 Penny doesn't never exercise.
6 Never I go swimming at night.
7 Vivian doesn't drink always coffee.
8 Corey and I play twice a week tennis together.
9 We go often bike riding in the afternoon.
10 She is every day late for class.

The past tense of <u>be</u>: form

Use <u>was</u> and <u>were</u> for affirmative statements. Use <u>wasn't</u> and <u>weren't</u> for negative statements.

I **was** in Rome yesterday.   They **were** in Paris.
She **wasn't** on time.   They **weren't** early.

Begin <u>yes</u> / <u>no</u> questions with <u>Was</u> or <u>Were</u>.

Was your flight late?   **Were** you late?

Begin information questions with a question word followed by <u>was</u> or <u>were</u>.

How long **was** your vacation?   How many people **were** there?
Where **was** your passport?   Where **were** your tickets?

A Complete the conversations with <u>was</u>, <u>were</u>, <u>wasn't</u>, or <u>weren't</u>.

1 **A:** .... you out of town last week?
   B: No, I .... Why?
   A: Well, you .... at work all week.

2 **A:** How .... the food?
   B: Great! There .... lots of fresh seafood, and
   the fruit .... delicious.

3 **A:** So .... your vacation OK?
   B: Well, actually it .... The food
   .... terrible, and there .... too
   many people.

4 **A:** Where .... you last weekend?
   B: I .... on vacation.
   A: Really? How .... it?

5 **A:** How long .... your trip?
   B: Only a few hours, but we .... pretty tired.

6 **A:** .... your brother on vacation last week?
   B: Yes, he .... He and his wife ....
   on a cruise.

B On a separate sheet of paper, unscramble the words to write questions, using <u>was</u> or <u>were</u>.

1 vacation / your / very long
2 your luggage / where
3 comfortable / the drive
4 you / on the morning flight
5 late / your friends
6 there / how many / on the train / people

The simple past tense: spelling rules for regular verbs

Form the past tense of most verbs by adding <u>-ed</u> to the base form.
   play ➔ play**ed**

For verbs ending in <u>-e</u> or <u>-ie</u>, add <u>-d</u>.
   smile ➔ smile**d**   tie ➔ tie**d**

For one-syllable verbs ending in one vowel + one consonant, double the consonant and add <u>-ed</u>.
   stop ➔ stop**ped**   plan ➔ plan**ned**

For two-syllable verbs ending in one vowel + one consonant: If the first syllable is stressed, add <u>-ed</u>.
   vi - sit ➔ visit**ed**

If the second syllable is stressed, double the consonant and add <u>-ed</u>.
   pre - fer ➔ prefer**red**

For verbs ending in a consonant and <u>-y</u>, change the <u>-y</u> to <u>-i</u> and add <u>-ed</u>.
   study ➔ stud**ied**

Be careful! Do not use <u>-ed</u> for irregular verbs.

See page 122 for a list of irregular verbs in the simple past tense form.

A Write the simple past tense form of the verbs.

1 return ....
2 like ....
3 change ....
4 cry ....

5 try ....
6 stay ....
7 travel ....
8 arrive ....

9 rain ....
10 wait ....
11 offer ....
12 hurry ....

B Write the simple past tense form of these irregular verbs.

1 eat ....
2 drink ....
3 swim ....
4 go ....

5 write ....
6 meet ....
7 run ....
8 begin ....

9 buy ....
10 read ....
11 pay ....
12 understand ....

The simple past tense: usage and form

Use the simple past tense to talk about completed actions in the past.
My grandparents **went** to Paris in April.
Last year, we **played** tennis and **did** aerobics every day.

Negative forms
Use <u>didn't</u> + the base form of a verb.
He **didn't go** out last weekend. NOT He didn't ~~went~~ out last weekend.
They **didn't have** a good time. NOT They didn't ~~had~~ a good time.

Questions
Begin <u>yes</u> / <u>no</u> questions with <u>Did</u>. Use the base form of the verb.
Did you **go** swimming every day? NOT Did you ~~went~~ swimming every day?

Begin information questions with a question word followed by <u>did</u>. Use the base form of the verb.
Where **did** you **go** shopping?   When **did** he **arrive**?   What **did** they **eat** every day?

C On a separate sheet of paper, change each affirmative statement into a negative statement.

1 I slept all night.
2 We went swimming.
3 She ate a lot of food.

4 They drank a lot of coffee.
5 We had dinner at eight.
6 He bought postcards.

D On a separate sheet of paper, unscramble the words to write questions. Use the simple past tense.

1 you / go / where / on vacation last summer
2 you / from vacation / get back / when
3 they / a good flight / have

4 in London / you / do / what
5 your parents / their trip / enjoy
6 stay / how long / in Paris / Alicia

UNIT 8 *Lesson 1*

Direct objects: usage

The subject of a sentence performs the action of the verb. A direct object receives the action of the verb.

subject	verb	direct object
I	like	**spicy food.**
Anne	wears	**dark clothes.**

A Underline the subjects in the sentences. Circle the direct objects.

1 <u>Stacey</u> is wearing a (bathrobe) right now.
2 Many people buy outerwear in this store.
3 I love red shoes.
4 Sanford and Gloria never wear shorts.

5 You can't enter this store before 10:00.
6 Do you have your credit card?
7 Marianne wants a pair of warm pajamas.

Indirect objects: usage rules and common errors

When a sentence contains a direct object and a prepositional phrase, you can use an indirect object to say the same thing.

prepositional phrase	indirect object
I'm buying the gloves **for her**.	I'm buying **her** the gloves.
Give the sweater **to Jay**.	Give **Jay** the sweater.

Be careful! When a sentence contains a prepositional phrase and a direct object, the direct object comes first.

Mindy wrote a letter to her parents. NOT Mindy wrote ~~to her parents a letter~~.

When a sentence contains a direct object and an indirect object, the indirect object comes first.

Mindy wrote **them** a letter. NOT Mindy wrote ~~a letter them~~.

B On a separate sheet of paper, rewrite each sentence, changing the prepositional phrase into an indirect object pronoun.

1 She buys clothes for them.
  She buys them clothes.

2 Laurie sends a check to her father every month.

3 At night we read stories to our children.

4 They serve meals to us in the dining room.

5 They never give gifts to me on my birthday.

C On a separate sheet of paper, rewrite each sentence, changing the indirect object pronoun into a prepositional phrase using the preposition in parentheses.

1 They never buy me dinner. (for)
  They never buy dinner for me.

2 He always gives me the check. (to)

3 I sent my colleagues the tickets. (to)

4 His friend showed him the check for dinner. (to)

5 She'd like to get her mother a book. (for)

D On a separate sheet of paper, rewrite the sentences, adding the indirect object or prepositional phrase to each sentence. *Don't add any words.*

1 They sent it on Monday. (to me)
  They sent it to me on Monday.

2 Did they give breakfast at the hotel? (you)

3 We always tell the truth. (her)

4 They make lunch every day. (for him)

5 He brought flowers last night. (his wife)

UNIT 8 *Lesson 2*

Comparative adjectives: spelling rules

Add -er to one-syllable adjectives. If the adjective ends in -e add -r.

tight ➔ tighter
loose ➔ looser

If an adjective ends in (or is) a consonant-vowel-consonant sequence, double the final consonant before adding -er.

hot ➔ hotter

For most adjectives that end in -y, change the y to i and add -er.

pretty ➔ prettier
busy ➔ busier

To make the comparative form of most adjectives that have more than two syllables, use more or less.

affordable ➔ **more affordable**
convenient ➔ **less convenient**

When comparing two people or things that are both in the sentence, use than when the second person or thing is mentioned.

She's less practical **than** her sister.
The weather is warmer there **than** here.

A On a separate sheet of paper, write the comparative form of the adjectives.

1 tall	**5** light	**9** sad	**13** spicy	**17** popular
2 sunny	**6** clean	**10** fatty	**14** healthy	**18** red
3 comfortable	**7** large	**11** salty	**15** cute	**19** conservative
4 heavy	**8** late	**12** sweet	**16** short	**20** interesting

B Complete each sentence with a comparative adjective. Use <u>than</u> if necessary.

1 I like the pink purse. It's much .... (nice).

2 Low-fat milk is not bad, but no-fat milk is .... (healthy).

3 France is .... (small) Russia.

4 Women's shoes are usually .... (expensive) men's shoes.

5 It's hot during the day, but it's .... (cool) at night.

6 He's a lot .... (tall) his brother.

7 This projector is a lot .... (popular), but it's .... (affordable).

8 They're much .... (liberal) about clothing rules at the beach.

9 It's usually .... (sunny) in the morning before the rain begins.

10 French fries are .... (fatty) and .... (salty) a salad.

UNIT 9 *Lesson 1*

Modals <u>can</u>, <u>could</u>, and <u>should</u>: meaning, form, and common errors

Meaning

Use <u>can</u> to express ability or possibility.

Jerome **can** speak Korean.   I **can** be there before 8:00.

Use <u>could</u> to offer an alternative or to make a weak suggestion.

They **could** see an old movie like *Titanic*, or they **could** go to something new.
You **could** eat a healthier diet.

Use <u>should</u> to give advice, to make a strong suggestion, or to express criticism.

You **should** think before you speak.

Form

Modals are followed by the base form of the main verb of the sentence, except in short answers to questions.

You **can eat** at a lot of good restaurants in this neighborhood.
Who **should read** this? They **should**.
Can you **see** the moon tonight? Yes, I **can**.

Use <u>not</u> between the modal and the base form.

You **shouldn't** stay at the Galaxy Hotel.   They **can't** take the express.

In <u>yes</u> / <u>no</u> questions, the modal precedes the subject of the sentence. In information questions, the question word precedes the modal.

Yes / no questions	Information questions
Should I buy a round-trip ticket?	When should they leave?
Can we make the 1:05 flight?	Why should they go?
Could she take an express train?	Which trains could I take?
	Who could they call?

> **BUT: Note the word order when <u>Who</u> is the subject.**
>
> Who can give me the information?
> (The travel agent can.)

Common errors

Never add <u>-s</u> to the third-person singular form of modals.

He **should buy** a ticket in advance. NOT ~~He shoulds buy~~ a ticket in advance.

Never use <u>to</u> between modals and the base form.

You **could take** the train or the bus. NOT You ~~could to take~~ the train or the bus.

Circle the correct phrases to complete the sentences.

1 Who (should buy / should to buy) the tickets?

2 Where (I can find / can I find) a hotel?

3 You (could to walk / could walk) or (take / taking) the bus.

4 (I should to call / Should I call) you when I arrive?

5 We (can to not take / can't take) the bus; it left.

6 When (should you giving / should you give) the agent your boarding pass?

7 Which trains (can get / can getting) me there soon?

UNIT 9 Lesson 2

Expansion: future actions

There are four ways to express future actions, using present forms.

Be going to

Be going to + base form usually expresses a future plan or certain knowledge about the future.

I'm going to spend my summer in Africa.   She's going to get a rental car when she arrives.
It's going to rain tomorrow.

The present continuous

The present continuous can also express a future plan.

We're traveling tonight.   They aren't wearing formal clothes to the wedding.
I'm not eating at home tomorrow.

The simple present tense

The simple present tense sometimes expresses a future action with verbs of motion: <u>arrive</u>, <u>come</u>, <u>depart</u>, <u>fly</u>, <u>go</u>, <u>leave</u>, <u>sail</u>, and <u>start</u>—especially when on a schedule or a timetable. When the simple present tense expresses the future, there is almost always a word, phrase, or clause indicating the future time.

This Monday, the express leaves at noon.   The flight arrives at 9:00 tonight.

The present of be

The present of <u>be</u> can describe a future event if it includes a word or phrase that indicates the future.

The wedding is on Sunday.

A Read the arrival and departure schedules. Then complete each sentence or question with the simple present tense.

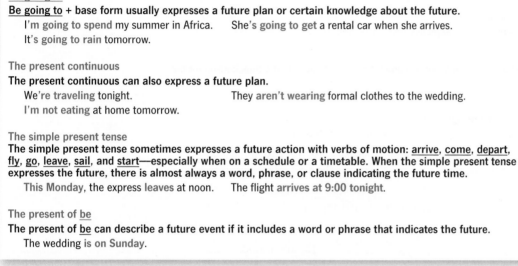

1 The bus .... at 11:00. It .... at 8:00.

2 A: When .... the flight ....?
   B: It .... at 23:30.

3 A: What time .... the train .... in Beijing?
   B: At 10:20 P.M.

4 A: .... the train .... at 7:00?
   B: Yes, it does.

B On a separate sheet of paper, answer each of the questions with a complete sentence. There may be more than one correct way to answer each question.

1 What are your plans for your next vacation?

2 What are you going to do this weekend?

3 What are you doing this evening?

Comparative and superlative adjectives: usage and form

Usage

Comparative adjectives compare two people, places, or things. Use <u>than</u> when the second item is mentioned.

Mexico City is **larger than** Los Angeles.

Compared with Los Angeles, Mexico City is **larger**.

Housing in New York is **more expensive than** in Lima.

Compared with Lima, housing is **more expensive** in New York.

Superlative adjectives compare more than two people, places, or things.

Compared to other cities in the Americas, Mexico City is **the largest**.

> **Be careful! Use <u>the</u> with superlative adjectives.**
>
> Don't say: Mexico City is ~~largest~~.

Form

adjective	comparative adjective	superlative adjective
cheap	cheaper (than)	the cheapest
expensive	more expensive (than)	the most expensive
practical	less practical (than)	the least practical

Superlative adjectives: spelling rules

Add <u>-est</u> to one-syllable adjectives. If the adjective ends in <u>-e</u>, add <u>-st</u>.

cheap → the cheapest   loose → the loosest

If an adjective ends in (or is) a consonant-vowel-consonant sequence, double the final consonant before adding <u>-est</u>.

hot → the hottest

For most adjectives that end in <u>-y</u>, change the y to i and add <u>-est</u>.

pretty → the prettiest   busy → the busiest

To form the superlative of most adjectives of two or more syllables, use <u>the most</u> or <u>the least</u>.

Car trips are **the least expensive** vacations.   Cruises are **the most relaxing** vacations.

A Write *both* the comparative and superlative form of each adjective.

		comparative	superlative			comparative	superlative
1	tall	....	....	10	interesting	....	....
2	easy	....	....	11	conservative	....	....
3	liberal	....	....	12	light	....	....
4	heavy	....	....	13	casual	....	....
5	unusual	....	....	14	comfortable	....	....
6	pretty	....	....	15	relaxing	....	....
7	exciting	....	....	16	long	....	....
8	wild	....	....	17	short	....	....
9	informal	....	....	18	scary	....	....

B Complete each sentence with a comparative or superlative adjective. Use <u>than</u> if necessary.

1 That dinner was .... (delicious) meal we had on our vacation.

2 The Caribbean cruise is .... (relaxing) of our vacation packages.

3 The Honsu X24 is a good camera, but the Cashio is .... (easy) to use.

4 We have several models, but I'd say the R300 is .... (popular).

5 I like that rug, but I think this one is .... (beautiful).

6 Our vacation in Brazil was .... (nice) our vacation in Italy last year.

7 All three stoves look good. But which one is .... (easy) to use?

8 I like both the J12, the Summit, and the Pro tablets, but which one's .... (small)?

9 Which of these three plates do you think is .... (pretty)?

10 I can't decide if I should read this book or that one. Which one is .... (interesting)?

Intensifiers *very*, *really*, and *too*

Intensifiers make the meaning of adjectives stronger.

<u>Very</u> and <u>really</u> have the same meaning. They can intensify adjectives with a positive or negative meaning.

That restaurant is really (or very) good. I want to go there.

That movie is really (or very) scary. I don't want to see it.

<u>Too</u> also makes the meaning of adjectives stronger. But <u>too</u> expresses the idea of "more than enough." <u>Too</u> usually has a negative meaning.

That movie is too long. I don't want to see it.

This restaurant is too expensive. I'm not going to eat here.

Be careful! **Don't use <u>too</u> to intensify adjectives with a positive meaning. Use <u>very</u> and <u>really</u>.**

This camera is very affordable! NOT This camera is ~~too affordable~~!

A Complete each sentence with <u>too</u>, <u>really</u>, or <u>very</u> and your own adjective.

1 Beach vacations are .... I love them.

2 French fries are .... You shouldn't eat them every day.

3 A cruise is .... I don't have enough money to take one.

4 They say this movie is .... I want to see it.

5 This book is .... You should read it.

6 English is .... People are learning it all over the world.

7 This printer is .... I need to replace it.

8 These pants are .... I need to buy a larger pair.

B Complete each conversation, using <u>too</u> or <u>enough</u>.

1 **A:** How about this? Should we buy it for your mother?

 B: No. It isn't .... (pretty). I want something nicer.

2 **A:** Do you think this rug is too small?

 B: No, it's great. I think it's .... (big).

3 **A:** Did you buy a microwave yesterday?

 B: I looked at some. But they were .... (expensive).

4 **A:** Why are you sending that steak back to the chef?

 B: It's an expensive meal, and this steak just isn't .... (good).

5 **A:** You never eat dessert?

 B: No. Desserts are .... (sweet) for me.

6 **A:** How was your vacation?

 B: To tell the truth, it just wasn't .... (relaxing).

7 **A:** How's that soup? Is it .... (hot)?

 B: No, it's fine. Thanks.

8 **A:** Would you like more ice in your water?

 B: Yes, please. It isn't .... (cold).

Writing Booster

The Writing Booster is optional. It is intended to teach students the conventions of written English. Each unit's Writing Booster is focused both on a skill and its application to the Writing exercise from the Unit Review page.

UNIT 1

Capitalization

Use a capital letter to begin a sentence.
Meet my new classmate. Her first name is Sue.

Use a capital letter for:

cities / countries	I live in Beijing. He's from Colombia.
nationalities	They're Honduran.
languages	I speak Russian and Italian.
days and months	My birthday is on Tuesday, June 19th.
the pronoun I	My brother and I are students.
names and formal titles	I'd like you to meet Mr. Smith.

A On a separate sheet of paper, rewrite each sentence, using correct capitalization.

1 please say hello to julio cueva from lima, peru.

2 my friend mr. lee is a computer programmer from korea.

3 he is brazilian, and his birthday is in october.

4 my classmate ms. silva is twenty-six years old.

5 miss wang teaches chinese to college students.

6 this monday john met his friend mr. abe.

7 when i travel, i need to use english.

B **Guidance for the Writing Exercise (on page 12)** Answer the questions below when you write about your classmate. Add more information if you can. Make sure you use capital letters correctly.

- What's your classmate's name?
- Does your classmate have a nickname?
- How old is your classmate?
- What's your classmate's occupation?
- What is your classmate's hometown?
- Is your classmate's hometown his or her birthplace?
- Who's your classmate's favorite actor?
- What's your classmate's favorite sport?

UNIT 2

The sentence

In English, a sentence is a group of words that expresses a complete thought. A sentence has a subject and a verb. When you write a sentence, begin with a capital letter and end with a period.

subject	verb	subject	verb
The play	is great.	She	loves music.

A Circle the subject and underline the verb in each sentence.

1 Her children like folk music.

2 I don't like big concerts.

3 My boyfriend loves classical music.

4 Their favorite musician is Esperanza Spaulding.

5 The play isn't very good.

B Write an ✗ next to the groups of words that are not sentences.

☐ 1 A theater fan.

☐ 2 The theater is down the street from the park.

☐ 3 And around the corner from the art gallery.

☐ 4 I listen to music in the shower.

☐ 5 Really loud concerts.

☐ 6 Downloading music.

C **Guidance for the Writing Exercise (on page 24)** Use the ideas as a guide to help you write five sentences about your musical tastes. Begin each sentence with a capital letter and end each sentence with a period. Be sure to use a subject and a verb in each sentence.

Ideas
- your favorite music
- your favorite artist
- when you listen to music
- where you buy music

UNIT 3

Combining sentences with and or but

And
Use <u>and</u> to combine two sentences if you want to add information. It's common, but not necessary, to use a comma before <u>and</u>.

> My cousin loves rock music, **and** she's a great dancer.

But
Use <u>but</u> to combine two sentences if you want to show a difference or contrast. It's common, but not necessary, to use a comma before <u>but</u>.

> My stepfather loves classical music, **but** I love rock.
> My niece loves Latin music, **but** my nephew doesn't.

Be careful! In traditional formal writing, writers avoid beginning sentences with <u>And</u> or <u>But</u>.

> Don't write: My cousin loves rock music. ~~And she's a great dancer.~~
> Don't write: My cousin loves rock music. ~~But I don't.~~

A On a separate sheet of paper, combine the sentences, using <u>and</u>.

1 My sister-in-law has long hair. She's very pretty.
2 My aunt is a computer programmer. Her husband is a teacher.
3 We look alike. We wear the same kind of clothes.
4 My cousin likes classical music. He loves Italian food.
5 We look very different. We like different music.

B On a separate sheet of paper, combine the sentences, using <u>but</u>.

1 My brother wears old clothes. I wear new clothes.
2 My sister has long hair. I have short hair.
3 My cousin lives near the airport. His parents don't.
4 I love rock music. My stepfather doesn't.
5 We look alike. We wear very different clothes.

C **Guidance for the Writing Exercise (on page 36)** Use the ideas to help you write the six statements comparing two people in your family. Use <u>and</u> or <u>but</u> to combine sentences.

Ideas
- appearance
- musical tastes
- food preferences
- clothing preferences
- birthplaces and hometowns
- marital status
- favorite colors

UNIT 4

Connecting words or ideas: and and in addition

And
Remember that <u>and</u> connects two sentences and makes them one sentence.

> I like fruit, **and** I also like vegetables.

You can also use <u>and</u> to connect words in a series. Notice the use of the comma in the examples below.

> I like apples, oranges, grapes, **and** other fruits.

Be careful! Don't use a comma when <u>and</u> connects only two words.

> I like apples and oranges. NOT I like ~~apples, and oranges.~~

In addition
<u>In addition</u> connects the ideas in one sentence with the ideas in the next sentence. Use a comma after <u>in addition</u>.

> I like fruit. **In addition,** I like vegetables.
> I like apples and oranges. **In addition,** I like grapes and other fruits.

A Connect the words and ideas with <u>and</u> or <u>in addition</u>.

1 The people eat a lot of vegetables in Spain, Italy, ... France.

2 In the U.S., many restaurants serve big portions. .... , they serve a lot of fatty foods.

3 There are five or six great Italian restaurants near the hotel. .... , there are two restaurants where the menu has dishes from Mexico, Thailand, India, ... even Indonesia!

4 She loves pasta, ... I want to invite her to my favorite Italian restaurant.

5 Raw carrots taste great, ... they're good for you.

6 This restaurant has great food. .... , the service is excellent.

7 You can choose from six entrées on the menu, ... they all come with a choice of vegetable.

8 I usually order soup, salad, a main course, ... dessert.

B **Guidance for the Writing Exercise (on page 48)** Read the description of food in the United States. Use these paragraphs as a guide to help you write the article about the food of your country. Change the details so the sentences describe your food.

> American food is more than hamburgers, hot dogs, and pancakes. The best American food is regional. One regional specialty is clam chowder. Clam chowder is a delicious soup from the northeast coast. In Boston, clam chowder contains milk, and in New York it contains tomatoes. Clam chowder always contains Atlantic clams. In addition, clam chowder always contains some vegetables, such as onions, potatoes, peppers, or corn.
>
> Another famous regional specialty of American cooking is barbecue. Barbecue comes from the center and south of the United States. Barbecue style is not always the same, but it always has meat and a spicy sauce. Americans are very proud of barbecue. Many restaurants claim that they have the only authentic barbecue. When you travel to the United States, be sure to try some regional specialties like clam chowder and barbecue.

UNIT 5

Placement of adjectives: before nouns and after the verb <u>be</u>

Adjectives are words that describe nouns and pronouns.

       noun   **pronoun**

The old photocopier is obsolete.   It's also broken.

Adjectives come before nouns or after the verb <u>be</u> when the subject of a sentence is a noun or pronoun.

I have a new computer.

The computer is new. It's terrific.

Be careful! Adjectives don't come after nouns. Adjectives don't have plural forms.

new refrigerators

NOT ~~refrigerators new~~

NOT ~~news refrigerators~~

When two adjectives describe the same noun, connect them with <u>and</u>. When there are more than two, use commas.

The microwave is popular and convenient.

This camera is obsolete, broken, and defective.

Adjectives	
affordable	good
awesome	great
awful	guaranteed
broken	new / old
convenient	obsolete
defective	popular
fast	terrible
fixable	terrific

Some adjectives are compound phrases.

This scanner is really up-to-date.

She bought an up-to-date camcorder.

A Circle the adjectives in each sentence.

1 My old printer is obsolete.

2 The XLM projector is easy to use. In addition, it's small and very portable.

3 Is your scanner fixable?

4 This terrible car is a lemon! It's awful.

5 Our new washing machine is both good and guaranteed.

B On a separate sheet of paper, write sentences about five of the following electronic devices or about other ones. Use the Adjectives from page 144.

Products

a smart phone	a desktop (computer)
a mobile / cell phone	a digital camera
a GPS	a TV
a tablet (computer)	a camcorder

> *My smart phone is very convenient.*

C **Guidance for the Writing Exercise (on page 60)** Use your answers to the questions below as a guide to help you write the review of a product you use. Give your product 1–5 stars.

- What is it?
- What brand is it?
- What model is it?
- Is it a good product? Why or why not?
- What does it do?

- What adjectives describe it?
- Where do you use it?
- Is it working?
- Does it drive you crazy?
- How old is it?

UNIT 6

Punctuation of statements and questions

Use a period at the end of a statement.
I go to the gym every morning.

Use a question mark at the end of a question.
What do I do to stay in shape?

Use an exclamation point at the end of a sentence if you want to indicate that something is funny or surprising.
The truth is I'm a couch potato!

> period = .
> question mark = ?
> exclamation point = !
> comma = ,
>
> **Remember:**
> **Use commas to connect more than two ideas in a series.**
> I go to the gym, go running in the park, and go bike riding every weekend.
>
> **It's common, but not necessary, to use a comma before <u>and</u> or <u>but</u> when you connect two ideas.**
> I eat well, but I don't exercise.

A On a separate sheet of paper, rewrite each statement or question, using correct punctuation. Remember to begin each with a capital letter.

1 I really don't have time to exercise
2 do you get enough sleep every night
3 my friends think I exercise a lot but I don't
4 we go running bike riding and swimming in the summer

5 my father never eats sweets but I do
6 what do I do on weekends
7 my younger brothers eat junk food watch TV and stay up late every night
8 am I a couch potato

B **Guidance for the Writing Exercise (on page 72)** Use the Ideas to write three questions with "I." Use these questions to introduce each topic in your description of your exercise and health habits. Be sure to check all your sentences and questions for correct punctuation.

> *What foods do I eat? I usually eat healthy foods during the week, but . . .*

Ideas
- the foods you eat
- the foods you avoid
- your exercise routine

Time order

Use a time clause in a sentence to show the order of events.
We visited the old part of town **after we had lunch**.
We checked into our hotel **before we had lunch**.

You can begin a sentence with a time clause. Most writers use a comma when the time clause comes first.
After we had lunch, we visited the old part of town.
Before we had lunch, we checked into our hotel.

Use transition signals to show time order in a paragraph. Use <u>First</u> to begin a series and <u>Finally</u> to end one. Use <u>Then</u>, <u>Next</u>, and <u>After that</u> to indicate a series of events. Commas are optional.
First, we checked in to our hotel. **After** we had lunch, we visited the old part of town and took pictures. **Then,** we went to the beach and lay in the sun for a while. **Next,** we played golf. **After that,** we went shopping and bought a rug. **Finally,** we went back to our hotel.

A On a separate sheet of paper, use the cues to write sentences. Begin each sentence with a time clause.

1 (before) First we had lunch. Then we went to the beach.
  Before we went to the beach, we had lunch

2 (after) First we visited Rome. Then we went to Venice.

3 (before) First they went snorkeling. After that, they had lunch.

4 (after) He arrived in Miami on Saturday. Then he looked for a hotel.

5 (before) I spent three days in Mexico City. Next I flew to Cancún.

6 (after) She got back from the airport. After that, she called her mother.

7 (before) The weather was beautiful. Then it rained.

B On a separate sheet of paper, rewrite the paragraph, using time-order transition words.

Let me tell you about my trip. I flew from New York to London, and I spent two days there. I took the train through the Chunnel to Paris. Paris was amazing. I got a car and drove to Rome. It was a long drive, but it was really scenic. I took a boat to the island of Sardinia. It was very beautiful. I flew back to London and back home to New York.

C **Guidance for the Writing Exercise (on page 84)** Write sentences describing your vacation in the order that the events happened. Then use your sentences to write your paragraph, using time clauses and time-order transition words.

UNIT 8

Connecting ideas with <u>because</u> and <u>since</u>

A clause with <u>because</u> or <u>since</u> presents a reason. There's no difference in meaning between <u>because</u> and <u>since</u> in the following sentences.
I'm going to Paris **because I love French food**.
He's not wearing a jacket **since it's really warm today**.

In speaking, it's OK to answer a question using only a clause with <u>because</u> or <u>since</u>.
A: Why are you wearing jeans?
B: **Because it's a really casual restaurant.**

In writing, however, a clause beginning with <u>because</u> or <u>since</u> is not a sentence; it's an incomplete thought. To make the thought complete, connect the clause beginning with <u>because</u> or <u>since</u> to a sentence.
I wear jeans at that restaurant because it is a really casual restaurant.

A clause with <u>because</u> or <u>since</u> can come at the beginning or the end of the sentence. When it comes at the beginning, use a comma. It's good writing style to vary placement so all sentences don't sound the same.
I eat vegetables every day **because they are healthy**.
Because they are healthy, I eat vegetables every day.

> **Remember:**
> In English, a sentence is a group of words containing a subject and a verb. It expresses a complete thought.

A On a separate sheet of paper, connect and rewrite the sentences, using clauses with either <u>because</u> or <u>since</u>. **Be careful!** Make sure the clause with <u>because</u> or <u>since</u> presents a reason.

1 I'm wearing a sweater. I feel cold.
2 She called her brother. It was his birthday.
3 He bought a blue blazer. He needed it for a business trip.

4 They didn't have a ticket for the concert. They stayed home.
5 Our printer is broken. We have to get a new one.

B On a separate sheet of paper, answer each question with a complete sentence containing a clause with <u>because</u> or <u>since</u>.

1 Why do you like dance music?

I like dance music because it is happy music.

2 Why are you studying English?
3 Why is a clothing store better than a clothing website?

4 Why do people like malls?
5 Why are running shoes more comfortable than formal shoes?

C **Guidance for the Writing Exercise (on page 96)** Write a list of at least five clothing do's and don'ts for appropriate dress in your country. Explain the reasons for the tips, using <u>because</u> and <u>since</u>. Use your sentences as a guide to help you write your letter or e-mail.

Don't wear jeans to formal restaurants because people here are generally pretty conservative.

UNIT 9

The paragraph

A paragraph is a group of sentences that relate to a topic or a theme. When your writing contains information about a variety of topics, it is convenient to divide your writing into separate paragraphs.

Traditionally, **the first word of a paragraph is indented**. (Sometimes new paragraphs, especially in books, are not indented. Instead, a separation is made by leaving a blank line space, as follows.)

In the writing model to the right, the first paragraph is about the U.S., and the second paragraph is about Tanzania. Dividing the writing into two paragraphs makes it easier to read and understand.

blank line space

Clothing customs in different countries

Clothing customs in the United States are generally liberal, although in some places people dress more formally than in others. For example, in casual social settings, the dress code is almost "anything goes," and, in the summer, it's not unusual for people to go to nice restaurants in shorts and sandals. In offices and formal restaurants, though, people generally dress more conservatively in all seasons of the year.

Far away in East Africa, on the other hand, clothing customs are much more conservative, especially for women. Women should keep their shoulders covered, even in hot weather, and sleeveless shirts are always inappropriate. Skirts and pants should go to below the knees. In cities, and for business, a lightweight suit is appropriate for both men and women.

A Write a check mark in the place or places where a new paragraph could or should start. Then, on a separate sheet of paper, copy the paragraphs, indenting each one.

Famous families

Jackie Chan is a movie star and singer from Hong Kong. His wife, Joan Lin, is an actress from Taiwan. They have a son, JC Chan. He's a singer and actor in the United States. Another famous family is the Williams family. Venus and Serena Williams are famous tennis players. Their mother's name is Oracene Price. Their father, Richard Williams, was their coach. Still another famous family is the Fernández family from Mexico. Vicente and Alejandro are father and son. They are both singers, and they are famous all over Latin America.

B Guidance for the Writing Exercise (on page 108) Use the Ideas and your answers to the questions below as a guide to help you write your two paragraphs.

Paragraph 1

Begin your paragraph with an opening statement, such as: *Last month, I went to ___.*

- Where did you go?
- What kind of transportation did you take?
- Were there any transportation problems? If so, what were they?
- When did you leave?
- Who did you travel with?
- What did you do when you were there?
- When did you get back?

Paragraph 2

Begin your next paragraph with an opening statement, such as: *On my next trip, . . .*

- Where are you going to go?
- What kind of transportation are you going to take?
- Do you think you are going to have transportation problems on your next trip? Why or why not?
- When are you leaving?
- Who are you traveling with?
- What are you going to do when you are there?
- When are you getting back?

UNIT 10

Connecting contradictory ideas: *even though*, *however*, *on the other hand*

Use <u>even though</u> to connect contradictory ideas in a sentence. (A comma is optional before <u>even though</u> when it comes at the end of the sentence.)

Bee Flowers is the most popular shop in town even though it's quite expensive.
You can bargain for low prices at Marty's, even though the service isn't very friendly.

Always use a comma if the clause that begins with <u>even though</u> comes first.

Even though it's quite expensive, Bee Flowers is the most popular shop in town.
Even though the service isn't very friendly, you can bargain for low prices at Marty's.

Use <u>however</u> or <u>on the other hand</u> at the beginning of a sentence to connect contradictory ideas from one sentence to another. Use a comma.

You can bargain for low prices at Marty's. However, the service isn't very friendly.
Bee Flowers is quite expensive. On the other hand, it's the most popular shop in town.

Be careful! Don't use <u>however</u> or <u>on the other hand</u> to combine clauses in a sentence.

Don't write: You can bargain for low prices at Marty's, ~~however the service isn't very friendly~~.

A On a separate sheet of paper, combine each pair of sentences into one sentence, using <u>even though</u> to begin each one.

1 You can find some good deals at the Savoy Hotel. Their rooms are the most expensive in town.
2 You can bargain for really low prices at the Old Market. It isn't the prettiest place to shop.
3 The Philcov X30 is easy to use and not too expensive. It isn't the most popular camera.
4 The prices of smart phones are getting lower every year. They can still be very expensive.
5 The Samson camcorder is the most professional camera you can buy. It isn't the lightest.

B Now rewrite the sentences, using <u>however</u> or <u>on the other hand</u>.

C Guidance for the Writing Exercise (on page 120) Write at least six sentences about places to shop in your town or city. Use <u>even though</u>, <u>however</u>, and <u>on the other hand</u>. Use your sentences to help you write your guide.

♪♫ Top Notch Pop Lyrics

▶ 1:16–1:17 **It's Nice To Meet You**
[Unit 1]
(CHORUS)
It's nice to meet you.
Good to meet you.
Pleasure to meet you.

What's your name?
My name is Mr. Johnson.
Please just call me Stan.
I'd like you to meet my wife, Mary Anne.

(CHORUS)

What do you do?
Actually, I'm a teacher
at the Children's Institute.
The little kids are really cute.
That sounds nice. Where are you from—
somewhere far or near?
As a matter of fact, Chicago is my
hometown.
Could you say that louder please?
How did you end up here?
My father was a salesman.
We moved all around.

(CHORUS)

Who is that?
Let me introduce you
to my new friend Eileen.
She's a chef and she's nineteen.

(CHORUS)

Good-bye. Take care.

▶ 1:35–1:36 **Going Out** [Unit 2]
Do you want to see a play?
What time does the play begin?
It starts at eight. Is that OK?
I'd love to go. I'll see you then.
I heard it got some good reviews.
Where's it playing? What's the show?
It's called "One Single Life to Lose."
I'll think about it. I don't know.

(CHORUS)
Everything will be all right
when you and I go out tonight.

When Thomas Soben gives his talk—
The famous chef? That's not for me!
The doors open at nine o'clock.
There's a movie we could see
at Smith and Second Avenue.
That's my favorite neighborhood!
I can't wait to be with you.
I can't wait to have some food.

(CHORUS)

We're going to have a good time.
Don't keep me up past my bedtime.
We'll make a date.
Tonight's the night.
It starts at eight.
The price is right!
I'm a fan of rock 'n' roll.

Classical is more my style.
I like blues and I like soul.
Bach and Mozart make me smile!
Around the corner and down the street.
That's the entrance to the park.
There's a place where we could meet.
I wouldn't go there after dark!

(CHORUS: 2 times)

▶ 2:18–2:19 **An Only Child** [Unit 3]
Let me see the photos of
your wife and family.
Who's that guy there, on the right,
next to the TV?
Is that your younger brother, John?
And who are those two?
Your sisters both look so alike.
Please tell me what they do.

(CHORUS)
I ask so many questions.
You just answer with a smile.
You have a large family,
but I am an only child.

How about your cousins now?
Please tell me something new.
Do they both play basketball?
You know that I do, too.

(CHORUS)

I don't have a brother,
but you have two or three.
You're all one big happy family.
I don't have a sister,
but you have older twins.
This is a game I can't ever win.
Do you have nieces and nephews,
and how many are there now?
Do they all like the same kinds of things?
Are they different somehow?

(CHORUS)

▶ 2:34–2:35 **The World Café** [Unit 4]
Is there something that you want?
Is there anything you need?
Have you made up your mind
what you want to eat?
Place your order now,
or do you need more time?
Why not start with some juice—
lemon, orange, or lime?
Some like it hot, some like it sweet,
some like it really spicy.
You may not like everything you eat,
but I think we're doing nicely.

(CHORUS)
I can understand every word you say.
Tonight we're speaking English at
The World Café.

I'll take the main course now.
I think I'll have the fish.

Does it come with the choice of another
dish?
Excuse me waiter, please—
I think I'm in the mood
for a little dessert, and the cake looks good.
Do you know? Are there any low-fat desserts
that we could try now?
I feel like having a bowl of fruit.
Do you have to say good-bye now?

(CHORUS)

Apples, oranges, cheese, and ham,
coffee, juice, milk, bread, and jam,
rice and beans, meat and potatoes,
eggs and ice cream,
grilled tomatoes—
That's the menu.
That's the list.
Is there anything I missed?

(CHORUS)

▶ 3:22–3:23 **It's Not Working Again**
[Unit 5]
Hi. I'm calling on my cell phone.
I need a little help with a fax machine.
It's not working, and it's pretty bad.
I feel like I've been had, if you know
what I mean.
I'm coming to the store right now.
Can you show me how to use it?
The front lid won't open.
When my cat's around,
it squeaks and makes a funny sound.

(CHORUS)
It's not working again.
It's driving me crazy.
It's not working again.

I called yesterday, and a guy named Jack
said,
"I'm busy right now, can I call you back?"
He didn't even ask me what was wrong
with it.
He didn't want to hear the short and
long of it.
I just bought the thing yesterday,
and it won't turn on so please don't say,
"I'm sorry to hear that.
That's a shame.
That's too bad."
It's all a game.

(CHORUS)

I'm not looking for a laptop computer
or an X340 or a PDA.
Just tell me what's wrong with my fax
machine
so I can say good-bye and be on my way.
It won't send a copy of my document.
The paper goes through, and it comes
out bent.
On second thought, it's guaranteed.
I want my money back—that's what I need.

(CHORUS: 2 times)

► 3:40–3:41 **A Typical Day** [Unit 6]

The Couch Potato sits around.
He eats junk food by the pound.
It's just a typical day.
Watching as the world goes by,
he's out of shape and wonders why.
It's just a typical day.

(CHORUS)
Every night he dreams that he's
skydiving through the air.
And sometimes you appear.
He says, "What are you doing here?"

He cleans the house and plays guitar,
takes a shower, drives the car.
It's just a typical day.
He watches TV all alone,
reads and sleeps, talks on the phone.
It's just a typical day.

(CHORUS)

I'm sorry.
Mr. Couch Potato's resting right now.
Can he call you back?
He usually lies down every day of the week,
and he always has to have a snack.
Now all his dreams are coming true.
He's making plans to be with you.
It's just a typical day.
He goes dancing once a week.
He's at the theater as we speak!
It's just a typical day.

(CHORUS)

► 4:20–4:21 **My Dream Vacation**
[Unit 7]

The ride was bumpy
and much too long.
It was pretty boring.
It felt so wrong.
I slept all night,
and it rained all day.
We left the road,
and we lost the way.
Then you came along
and you took my hand.
You whispered words
I could understand.

(CHORUS)
On my dream vacation,
I dream of you.
I don't ever want to wake up.
On my dream vacation,
this much is true:
I don't ever want it to stop.

The food was awful.
They stole my purse.
The whole two weeks went
from bad to worse.
They canceled my ticket.
missed my flight.
were so unfriendly
wasn't right.
ed a taxi,
inside,

and there you were,
sitting by my side.

(CHORUS)

You were so unusual.
The day was so exciting.
I opened up my eyes,
and you were gone.
I waited for hours.
You never called.
I watched TV
and looked at the walls.
Where did you go to?
Why weren't you near?
Did you have a reason
to disappear?
So I flew a plane
to the south of France,
and I heard you say,
Would you like to dance?"

(CHORUS)

► 4:41–4:42 **Anything Goes** [Unit 8]

The shoe department's upstairs.
It's on the second floor.
Women's Casual is down the stairs,
there by the door.
This helpful store directory
shows every kind of clothes.
I look for the department where
it says anything goes.

(CHORUS)
At home and when I travel,
I always like to wear
pajamas in the daytime
with a blazer and a pair
of socks on my fingers
and gloves on my toes—
anything goes.

On the ground floor, there's a restaurant
and a photo studio,
so I take the escalator
down to the floor below.
There are turtlenecks and T-shirts.
There are cardigans and jeans
in every size and color.
They look comfortable and clean.

(CHORUS)

The salesperson says,
"Here you go.
Try it on.
That's not too bad.
Let me see if I can find you something
better."
Some people say that black clothes
are more flattering than white,
or they think that they look nicer
in the day or in the night.
Their clothes can't be too liberal
or too conservative.
If I love it, then I wear it.
That's the way I want to live.

(CHORUS)

► 5:21–5:22 **Five Hundred Ways**
[Unit 9]

You could take the bus,
or you could take the train.
You could take the ferry,
or you could take a plane.
Baby, it's a small world,
when all is said and done.
We have so many options,
the question is, which one?

(CHORUS)
There are five hundred ways to get here.
What are you going to do?
You could get a one-way ticket to see me.
I'm waiting here for you.

You should really hurry.
When are you going to call
and make your reservation?
You could miss them all.
And do you know how long
you are going to stay?
You could come and be with me
forever and a day.

(CHORUS)

Follow me.
Follow me.
Yes, you can follow me.
You have my phone number,
and you have my address.
Tell me, are you coming on
the local or express?

(CHORUS)

► 5:39–5:40 **Shopping for Souvenirs**
[Unit 10]

I go to the bank at a quarter to ten.
I pick up my cash from the ATM.
Here at the store, it won't be too hard
to take out a check or a credit card.
The bank has a good rate of exchange,
and everything here is in my price range.
The easiest part of this bargain hunt
is that I can afford anything I want.

(CHORUS)
Whenever I travel around the world,
I spend my money for two.
Shopping for souvenirs
helps me to be near you.

I try to decide how much I should pay
for the beautiful art I see on display.
To get a great deal, I can't be too nice.
It can't hurt to ask for a better price.

(CHORUS)

Yes, it's gorgeous, and I love it.
It's the biggest and the best,
though it might not be the cheapest.
How much is it—more than all the rest?
I'll pass on some good advice to you:
When you're in Rome, do as the Romans do.
A ten percent tip for the taxi fare
should be good enough when you're staying
there.

(CHORUS)